Table of Contents

I. Foreword 1

II. Executive Summary 3

III. Introduction 5

    Genesis of this Report 5

    Central Focus in 2012 6

    Overview of Standards-Related Measures 6

IV. Overview of Trade Obligations on Standards-Related Measures 9

    WTO Agreement on Technical Barriers to Trade 9

    Operation of the TBT Agreement 12

    Standards-Related Provisions in U.S. Free Trade Agreements 15

V. U.S. Statutory and Administrative Framework for Implementing Standards-Related Trade Obligations 19

VI. Standards 23

VII. Conformity Assessment Procedures 27

VIII. U.S. Processes for Identifying Standards-Related Trade Barriers and Determining How to Address Them 29

    Engagement in Voluntary Standards Activities 31

IX. U.S. Engagement on Standards-Related Measures in International, Regional, and Bilateral Fora 33

    Overview of U.S. Engagement on Standards-Related Measures 33

    WTO TBT Committee and Related Engagement 34

        Specific Trade Concerns 34

        Systemic Issues 35

    Total Economic Engagement Program 35

    Asia Pacific Economic Cooperation 36

        Good Regulatory Practices 36

	Smart Grid	37
	Green Buildings	37
	Solar Technologies	38
	Information and Communication Technologies	38
	APEC Food Safety Cooperation Forum (FSCF) and Partnership Training Institute Network (PTIN)	38
	Wine Regulatory Forum	39
	Global Food Safety Partnership	39
	Trans-Pacific Partnership	39
	Free Trade Agreement – TBT Committee Meetings	40
	Regulatory Cooperation Fora	40
	Executive Order 13609	40
	European Union	41
	Mexico	41
	Canada	42
	North American Leaders Summit – Trilateral Regulatory Cooperation	42
	Doha Round Negotiations	42
X.	2012-2013 Trends Regarding Standards-Related Measures	45
	Nutritional Labeling and Advertising	45
	EU Agreements on Conformity Assessment and Acceptance (ACAA)	45
	Voluntary" Measures as Trade Barriers	46
	Mandatory Labeling of Foods Derived from Genetic Engineering	47
XI.	Country Reports	49
	Background on Specific Trade Concerns Contained in the Country Reports	49
	Argentina	49
	Brazil	50

	Chile	52
	China	53
	Colombia	60
	The European Union	61
	India	65
	Indonesia	67
	Japan	69
	Kenya	70
	Korea	70
	Malaysia	73
	Mexico	74
	Russian Federation	76
	South Africa	79
	Taiwan	79
	Turkey	81
	Vietnam	82
XII.	Appendix A: List of Commenters	83
XIII.	Appendix B: List of Frequently Used Abbreviations and Acronyms	85

I. Foreword

This year the Office of the United States Trade Representative (USTR) publishes its fourth annual Report on Technical Barriers to Trade (TBT Report). This report was created to respond to the concerns of U.S. companies, farmers, ranchers, and manufacturers, which increasingly encounter non-tariff trade barriers in the form of product standards, testing requirements, and other technical requirements as they seek to sell products and services around the world. As tariff barriers to industrial and agricultural trade have fallen, standards-related measures of this kind have emerged as a key concern.

Governments, market participants, and other entities can use standards-related measures as an effective and efficient means of achieving legitimate commercial and policy objectives. But when standards-related measures are outdated, overly burdensome, discriminatory, or otherwise inappropriate, these measures can reduce competition, stifle innovation, and create unnecessary technical barriers to trade. These kinds of measures can pose a particular problem for small- and medium-sized enterprises (SMEs), which often do not have the resources to address these problems on their own. USTR is committed to identifying and combating unwarranted technical barriers to U.S. exports, many of which are detailed in this report. USTR's efforts to prevent and remove foreign technical barriers serve the President's goal of doubling U.S. exports by the end of 2014 through the National Export Initiative.

Since the last TBT Report was released, the United States has significantly advanced its efforts to resolve concerns with standards-related measures that act as unjustifiable barriers to trade and to prevent their emergence. USTR will continue its work to resolve and prevent trade concerns arising from standards-related measures *inter alia* through new and existing cooperative initiatives regarding standards-related issues in the World Trade Organization (WTO), Asia-Pacific Economic Cooperation Forum (APEC), U.S. free trade agreements (FTAs), and other bilateral fora, as well as progress on the negotiation of a modernized Technical Barriers to Trade (TBT) chapter in the Trans-Pacific Partnership (TPP) that will build on and strengthen TBT disciplines contained in the WTO Agreement on Technical Barriers to Trade (TBT Agreement). In addition, on February 13, 2013, President Obama and EU leaders announced that they would initiate the internal procedures necessary to launch negotiations on a comprehensive trade and investment agreement, the Transatlantic Trade and Investment Partnership. As conveyed in the February 2013 U.S.-EU High Level Working Group on Jobs and Growth (HLWG) Final Report, the United States and the EU are committed to working together to open markets in goods, services and investment, reduce non-tariff barriers, and address global trade issues of common concern. Both parties seek to build on the horizontal disciplines of the WTO TBT Agreement, establish ongoing mechanisms for improved dialogue and cooperation for addressing bilateral TBT issues, and pursue opportunities for greater regulatory compatibility with the objective of reducing costs stemming from regulatory differences in specific sectors.

Again in 2013, USTR will engage vigorously with other agencies of the U.S. Government, as well as interested stakeholders, to press for tangible progress by U.S. trading partners in removing unwarranted or overly burdensome technical barriers. We will fully utilize our toolkit of bilateral, regional and multilateral agreements and mechanisms in order to dismantle unjustifiable barriers to safe, high-quality U.S. industrial, consumer, and agricultural exports and strengthen the rules-based trading system. Recognizing that U.S. economic and employment recovery and growth continue to rely importantly on the strength of U.S. exports of goods, services, and agricultural products, we will be redoubling our efforts to ensure that the technical barriers that inhibit those exports are steadily diminished.

Ambassador Demetrios Marantis
Acting U.S. Trade Representative
April 2013

II. Executive Summary

The *2013 Report on Technical Barriers to Trade (TBT Report)* is a specialized report focused on significant foreign trade barriers in the form of product standards, technical regulations and testing, certification, and other procedures involved in determining whether products conform to standards and technical regulations and actions the United States is taking to address these barriers. These standards-related trade measures, which in World Trade Organization (WTO) terminology are known as "technical barriers to trade" (TBT) when they act as barriers to trade, play a critical role in shaping the flow of global trade.

Standards-related measures serve an important function in facilitating international trade, including by enabling small and medium-sized enterprises (SMEs) to obtain greater access to foreign markets. Standards-related measures also enable governments to pursue legitimate objectives such as protecting human health and the environment and preventing deceptive practices. But standards-related measures that are non-transparent, discriminatory, or otherwise unwarranted can act as significant barriers to U.S. trade. Such measures can pose a particular problem for SMEs, which often do not have the resources to address these problems on their own.

This report describes and advances U.S. efforts to identify and eliminate standards-related measures that act as significant barrier to U.S. trade. The report consists of following key components:

- An introduction to standards-related measures, including the genesis of this report and the growing importance of standards-related measures in international trade (Section III);[1]

- An overview of standards-related trade obligations, in particular rules governing standards-related measures under the WTO Agreement on Technical Barriers to Trade (TBT Agreement) and U.S. free trade agreements (Section IV);

- A description of the U.S. legal framework for implementing its standards-related trade obligations (Section V);

- A discussion of standards, including the role of international standards in facilitating trade and fulfilling legitimate public policy objectives and federal agencies' participation in standards development (Section VI);

---

[1] For readers seeking a deeper understanding of the specific topics covered in this report, references and hyperlinks to additional information are provided throughout the report. To access official documents of the WTO (such as those identified by the document symbol "G/TBT/...") click on "simple search" and enter the document symbol at the WTO's document retrieval website: *http://docsonline.wto.org/gen_search.asp?searchmode=simple*.

- An elaboration on conformity assessment procedures, including federal agencies' use of conformity assessment and the possibility for international systems of conformity assessment to facilitate trade (Section VII);

- A description of how the U.S. Government identifies technical barriers to trade and the process of interagency and stakeholder consultation it employs to determine how to address them (Section VIII);

- An explanation of how the United States engages with its trading partners to address standards-related measures that act as barriers and prevent creation of new barriers through multilateral, regional, and bilateral channels, including the WTO's Committee on Technical Barriers to Trade (TBT Committee) and cooperative activities under the APEC Subcommittee on Standards and Conformance, among others (Section IX);

- A summary of current trends regarding standards-related measures trends relating to standards-related measures (Section X); and

- An identification and description of significant standards-related trade barriers currently facing U.S. exporters, along with U.S. government initiatives to eliminate or reduce the impact of these barriers (Section XI) in 17countries – Argentina, Brazil, China, Chile, Colombia, India, Indonesia, Japan, Kenya, Korea, Malaysia, Mexico, Russia, South Africa, Taiwan, Turkey, and Vietnam – as well as the European Union (EU).

III. Introduction

Genesis of this Report

Shortly after taking office in 2009, President Obama reaffirmed America's commitment to ensuring the effective implementation and enforcement of the WTO's system of multilateral trade rules. The President vowed to pursue an aggressive and transparent program of defending U.S. rights and benefits under the rules-based trading system as a key element in his vision to restore trade's role in leading economic growth and promoting higher living standards. The President has also recognized that non-tariff barriers have grown in significance for U.S. exporters seeking access to foreign markets. Two kinds of non-tariff measures pose a particular challenge to U.S. exports: sanitary and phytosanitary (SPS) measures and standards-related measures.

Accordingly, in 2009 U.S. Trade Representative Ambassador Kirk directed the Office of the U.S. Trade Representative (USTR) to create a new *Report on Sanitary and Phytosanitary Measures (SPS Report)* and a *Report on Technical Barriers to Trade (TBT Report)*. He directed USTR staff to use these reports to promote understanding of the process of identifying non-tariff measures that act as significant barriers to U.S. exports; to provide a central focus for engagement by U.S. agencies in resolving trade concerns related to non-tariff barriers; and to document the actions underway to give greater transparency and confidence to American workers, producers, businesses, and other stakeholders regarding the actions this Administration is taking on their behalf.

The *TBT Report* is a specialized report addressing significant foreign barriers in the form of product standards, technical regulations, and conformity assessment procedures (standards-related measures). Prior to 2010, the *National Trade Estimate Report on Foreign Trade Barriers (NTE Report)* addressed standards-related measures.[2] By addressing significant foreign trade barriers in the form of standards-related measures, the *TBT Report* meets the requirements under Section 181 of the Trade Act of 1974, as amended, to report on significant foreign trade barriers with respect to standards-related measures. A separate report addressing significant foreign trade barriers in the form of SPS measures (*2013 Report on Sanitary and Phytosanitary Measures*) is being released in parallel to this report.

The *TBT Report* includes country reports that identify specific standards-related trade barriers imposed or under consideration by certain U.S. trading partners. The report also includes general information on standards-related measures, the processes and procedures the United States uses to implement these measures domestically, and the tools the United States uses to

---

[2] In accordance with section 181 of the Trade Act of 1974 (the 1974 Trade Act) (codified at 19 U.S.C. § 2241), as amended by section 303 of the Trade and Tariff Act of 1984 (the 1984 Trade Act), section 1304 of the Omnibus Trade and Competitiveness Act of 1988 (the 1988 Trade Act), section 311 of the Uruguay Round Trade Agreements Act (1994 Trade Act), and section 1202 of the Internet Tax Freedom Act, the Office of the U.S. Trade Representative is required to submit to the President, the Senate Finance Committee, and appropriate committees in the House of Representatives, an annual report on significant foreign trade barriers. The statute requires an inventory of the most important foreign barriers affecting U.S. exports of goods and services, foreign direct investment by U.S. persons, and protection of intellectual property rights.

address standards-related measures when they act as unnecessary barriers to trade. This general information is provided to assist the reader in understanding the issues and trade concerns described in the last two sections of the report, as well as the channels for resolving them. These last two sections review current trends relating to standards-related measures that can have a significant impact on trade and identify and describe significant standards-related trade barriers currently facing U.S. producers and businesses, along with U.S. government initiatives to eliminate or reduce these barriers.

Like the *NTE Report,* the source of the information for the *TBT Report* includes stakeholder comments that USTR solicited through a notice published in the *Federal Register*, reports from U.S. embassies abroad and from other Federal agencies, and USTR's ongoing consultations with domestic stakeholders and trading partners. An appendix to this report includes a list of commenters that submitted comments in response to the *Federal Register* notice.

Central Focus in 2012

During 2012, the United States succeeded in persuading its trading partners to reduce or eliminate a variety of technical barriers to trade identified in last year's report. The United States also continued to intensify its efforts to help other governments to avoid imposing unwarranted standards-related barriers to trade, particularly with respect to innovative technologies and new areas of regulation, and to strengthen their capacity to regulate properly and to promote good regulatory practices. In 2012, the United States also proposed new initiatives in key trade and economic forums, including in the WTO and the Asia-Pacific Economic Cooperation Forum (APEC), as well as in negotiations to conclude a Trans-Pacific Partnership (TPP) agreement, to encourage governments to eliminate and prevent unwarranted standards-related barriers to trade.

Overview of Standards-Related Measures

Today, standards-related measures (standards, technical regulations, and conformity assessment procedures) play a critical role in shaping the flow of international trade. While tariffs still constitute an important source of distortions and economic costs, the relative role of tariffs in shaping international trade has declined due in large part to successful rounds of multilateral tariff reductions in the WTO and its predecessor, the General Agreement on Tariffs and Trade (GATT 1947). With these declines in tariffs, the role of non-tariff barriers in international trade has become more prominent.

Broadly speaking, standards-related measures are documents and procedures that set out specific technical or other requirements for products or processes as well as procedures to ensure that these requirements are met. Among other things standards-related measures help:

- ensure the connectivity and compatibility of inputs sourced in different markets;

- manage the flow of product-related information through complex and increasingly global supply chains;

- organize manufacturing or other production processes around replicable routines and procedures to yield greater product quality assurance;

- achieve important regulatory and societal objectives, such as ensuring product safety, preventing deceptive practices, and protecting the environment; and

- promote more environmentally-sound or socially-conscious production methods.

Standards-related measures also play a vital role in enabling greater competition by conveying information to producers and consumers about the characteristics or performance of components and end products they purchase from a wide variety of suppliers. These measures also enable more widespread access to technical innovations. Standards-related measures can offer particularly pronounced benefits to SMEs from this perspective. Uniform standards and product testing procedures established under a common set of technical requirements that producers can rely on in manufacturing components and end products, can facilitate the diffusion of technology and innovation, contribute to increasing buyer-seller confidence, and assist SMEs to participate in global supply chains.

Conversely, outdated, overly burdensome, discriminatory, or otherwise inappropriate standards-related measures can reduce competition, stifle innovation, and create unnecessary obstacles to trade. Even when standards-related measures are used appropriately, firms – particularly SMEs – can face significant challenges in accessing information about, and complying with, diverse and evolving technical requirements in major export markets. This is particularly the case when technical requirements change rapidly or differ markedly across markets.

Thus, while standards-related measures can be an effective and efficient means of achieving legitimate commercial and policy objectives, policy makers, industry officials, and other stakeholders must also confront an important question: how to ensure that standards-related measures facilitate innovation, competition, consumer and environmental protection, and other public policy objectives – without creating unnecessary obstacles to trade? As supply chains grow increasingly complex, governments and other stakeholders must also address the question of how to better align standards and technical requirements across jurisdictions and markets as a means to facilitate the flow of goods across borders, reduce costs associated with complying with different standards and technical regulations across jurisdictions and markets, and enhance governments' ability to achieve important public policy objectives.

The rules, procedures, and opportunities for engagement that international, regional, and bilateral trade agreements establish serve as an important foundation for addressing many of these questions. The TBT Agreement is the principal agreement establishing multilateral rules governing standards-related measures. (Box 1 lays out definitions provided under the TBT Agreement for standards-related measures.) U.S. free trade agreements (FTAs) establish additional rules with respect to these measures with specific trading partners. The TBT Agreement's rules are vital in setting the terms on which the United States engages with its trading partners on standards-related measures, and U.S. FTAs build on these rules in important ways. These agreements are described in more detail in Section IV below.

A broad and active agenda of U.S. engagement on many fronts is needed to ensure that foreign standards-related measures do not impose unwarranted barriers to trade. USTR leads Federal government policy deliberations on these measures through the interagency Trade Policy Staff Committee (TPSC).[3] U.S. activities in the WTO are at the forefront of USTR's efforts to prevent and resolve trade concerns arising from standards-related measures. Coordinating with relevant agencies through the TPSC, USTR engages with other governments in many venues, including those established by U.S. FTAs and through regional and multilateral organizations, such as the WTO, APEC and the Organization for Economic Cooperation and Development (OECD). USTR also raises standards-related issues in bilateral dialogues with U.S. trading partners. These efforts are designed to ensure that U.S. trading partners adhere to internationally-agreed rules governing these measures and to reduce or eliminate unnecessary measures of this kind that can create barriers for U.S. producers and businesses.

Box 1. Key Definitions in the WTO Agreement on Technical Barriers to Trade

Technical regulation

> Document which lays down product characteristics or their related processes and production methods, including the applicable administrative provisions, with which compliance is mandatory. It may also include or deal exclusively with terminology, symbols, packaging, marking, or labeling requirements as they apply to a product, process, or production method.

Standard

> Document approved by a recognized body, that provides, for common and repeated use, rules, guidelines, or characteristics for products or related processes and production methods, with which compliance is not mandatory. It may also include or deal exclusively with terminology, symbols, packaging, marking, or labeling requirements as they apply to a product, process, or production method.

Conformity assessment procedures

> Any procedure used, directly or indirectly, to determine that relevant requirements in technical regulations or standards are fulfilled.
>
> *Explanatory note:* Conformity assessment procedures include, *inter alia*, procedures for sampling, testing and inspection; evaluation, verification and assurance of conformity; registration, accreditation, and approval as well as their combinations.

Source: Annex 1 of the TBT Agreement.

Note: These definitions apply only with respect to products and related processes and production methods, not to services.

---

[3] http://www.ustr.gov/about-us/executive-branch-agencies-trade-policy-staff-committee-and-trade-policy-review-group

IV. Overview of Trade Obligations on Standards-Related Measures

WTO Agreement on Technical Barriers to Trade

The WTO Agreement on Technical Barriers to Trade (TBT Agreement) contains rules that help ensure that standards-related measures serve legitimate objectives, are transparent, and do not create unnecessary obstacles to trade.[4] The TBT Agreement establishes rules on developing, adopting, and applying voluntary product standards and mandatory technical regulations as well as conformity assessment procedures (such as testing or certification) used to determine whether a particular product meets such standards or regulations. These rules help distinguish legitimate standards-related measures from protectionist measures, and ensure that testing and other conformity assessment procedures are fair and reasonable.

The TBT Agreement recognizes that WTO Members have the right to prepare, adopt, and apply standards-related measures necessary to protect human health, safety and the environment at the levels they consider appropriate and to achieve other legitimate objectives. At the same time, the TBT Agreement imposes obligations regarding the development and application of those measures. For example, the TBT Agreement requires governments to develop standards-related measures through transparent processes, and to base these measures on relevant international standards (where effective and appropriate). The TBT Agreement also prohibits measures that discriminate against imported products or create unnecessary obstacles to trade. The TBT Agreement contains a *Code of Good Practice for the Preparation, Adoption, and Application of Standards* (Code). The Code applies to the preparation, adoption, and application of voluntary standards and is open to acceptance by any standardizing body located in the territory of any WTO Member, including government and non-governmental bodies. Box 2 outlines the key disciplines of the TBT Agreement.

Box 2. Key principles and provisions of the TBT Agreement

Non-discrimination: The TBT Agreement states that "in respect of their technical regulations, products imported from the territory of any Member [shall] be accorded treatment no less favorable than that accorded to like products of national origin and to like products originating in any other country." (Art. 2.1) The Agreement requires Members to ensure that "conformity assessment procedures are prepared, adopted and applied so as to grant access for suppliers of like products originating in the territories of other Members under conditions no less favorable than those accorded to suppliers of like products of national origin or originating in any other country, in a comparable situation." (Art. 5.1.1) The Agreement also requires that Members ensure that related fees are equitable (Art. 5.2.5) and that they respect the confidentiality of information about the results of conformity assessment procedures for imported products in the same way they do for domestic products. (Art. 5.2.4)

Avoidance of unnecessary obstacles to trade: When preparing or applying a technical regulation, a Member must ensure that the regulation is not more trade-restrictive than necessary to fulfill the Member's legitimate objective. (Art. 2.2) The obligation to avoid unnecessary obstacles to trade applies also to conformity assessment procedures. They must not be stricter than necessary to provide adequate confidence that products conform to the applicable requirements. (Art. 5.1.2)

---

[4] http://www.wto.org/english/docs_e/legal_e/17-tbt_e.htm

Better alignment of technical regulations, standards, and conformity assessment procedures: The Agreement calls on Members to use relevant international standards, or the relevant parts of them, as a basis for their technical regulations, and to use relevant international recommendations and guides, or relevant portions of them, as the basis for their conformity assessment procedures. The Agreement, however, does not require the use of relevant international standards, guides and recommendations if they would be ineffective or inappropriate to fulfill the Member's "legitimate objectives." (Arts. 2.4 and 5.4) In addition, Members should participate "within the limits of their resources" in the preparation by international standardization bodies, of international standards for products for which they either have adopted, or expect to adopt, technical regulation, and in the elaboration of international guides and recommendations for conformity assessment procedures. (Art.2.6 and 5.5)

Use of performance-based requirements: Whenever appropriate, product requirements should be set in terms of *performance* rather than design or descriptive characteristics. (Art. 2.8)

International systems of conformity assessment: Members shall, whenever practicable, formulate and adopt international systems for conformity assessment and become members thereof or participate therein. (Art. 9.1)

Acceptance of technical regulations as equivalent: Alongside promoting better alignment of technical regulations, the Agreement encourages Members to accept technical regulations that other Members adopt as "equivalent" to their own if these regulations adequately fulfill the objectives of their own regulations. (Art. 2.7)

Mutual recognition of conformity assessment: The Agreement requires each Member to recognize "whenever possible" the results of conformity assessment procedures (*e.g.* test results or certifications), provided the Member is satisfied that those procedures offer an assurance of conformity that is equivalent as its own. (Art. 6.1) (Without such recognition, products might have to be tested twice, first by the exporting country and then by the importing country.) The Agreement recognizes that Members may need to consult in advance to arrive at a "mutually satisfactory understanding" regarding the competences of their respective conformity assessment bodies. (Art. 6.1) The Agreement also encourages Members to enter into negotiations to conclude agreements providing for the mutual recognition of each other's conformity assessment results (i.e., mutual recognition agreements or MRAs). (Art. 6.3)

Transparency: To help ensure transparency, the Agreement requires Members to publish a notice at an early stage and notify other Members through the WTO Secretariat when it proposes to adopt a technical regulation or conformity assessment procedure and to include in the notification a brief indication of the purpose of the proposed measure. These obligations apply whenever a relevant international standard, guide, or recommendation does not exist or the technical content of a proposed technical regulation or conformity assessment procedure is not in accordance with the technical content of relevant international standards, guides, or recommendations. In such circumstances, Members must allow "reasonable time" for other Members to comment on proposed technical regulations and conformity assessment procedures, which the TBT Committee has recommended be "at least 60 days" (G/TBT/26), and take comments it receives from other Members into account. (Art. 2.9 and 5.6) The Agreement establishes a Code of Good Practice that is applicable to voluntary standards and directs Members and standardizing bodies that have accepted it to publish every six months a work program containing the standards it is currently preparing and give interested parties at least 60 days to comment on a draft standard; once the standard is adopted it must be promptly published. (Annex 3) The Agreement also requires that all final technical regulations and conformity assessment procedures be promptly published. (Art. 2.11 and 5.8) In addition, the Agreement requires each Member to establish an inquiry point to answer all reasonable questions from other Members and interested parties and to provide documents relating to technical regulations, standards, and conformity assessment procedures adopted or proposed within its territory. (Art. 10.1)

Technical assistance: The Agreement calls on Members to provide technical assistance to other Members. (Art. 11) Technical assistance can be provided to help developing country Members with respect to such matters as preparing technical regulations, establishing national standardizing bodies, participating in international standardization bodies, and establishing bodies to assess conformity with technical regulations.

Enforcement and dispute settlement: The Agreement establishes the *Committee on Technical Barriers to Trade* as the major forum for WTO Members to consult on matters relating to the operation of the Agreement, including specific trade concerns about measures that Members have proposed or adopted. (Art. 13) The TBT Agreement

> provides for disputes under the Agreement to be resolved under the auspices of the WTO Dispute Settlement Body and in accordance with the terms of the WTO's Dispute Settlement Understanding. (Art. 14)
>
> **Other**: As noted above, the Agreement sets out a "Code of Good Practice" for preparing, adopting, and applying voluntary standards. (Annex 3) Standardizing bodies that Members establish at the central level of government must comply with the Code, and Members must take reasonable measures to ensure that local government and private sector standardizing bodies within their territories also accept and comply with the Code. (Art. 4.1) The Code is open to acceptance by any standardizing body in the territory of a WTO Member, including private sector bodies as well as public sector bodies. The Code requires Members and other standardizing bodies that have accepted it to adhere to obligations similar to those for technical regulations, for example, to ensure that the standards they adopt do not create unnecessary obstacles to trade and are based on relevant international standards, except where ineffective or inappropriate.
>
> Note: The OECD and WTO have also developed summaries of the TBT Agreement. See Trade Policy Working Paper No. 58, *Do Bilateral and Regional Approaches for Reducing Technical Barriers to Trade Converge Towards The Multilateral Trading System?* (OECD (TAD/TC/WP(2007)12/FINAL), WTO Trade Gateway, and TBT Committee reports and recommendations.

Access to information on product-related technical requirements is critical for facilitating trade. Producers, growers, manufacturers, and other supply chain participants need to know the requirements with which their products must comply in order to sell them in prospective markets. The TBT Agreement, therefore, requires every WTO Member to establish a national inquiry point that is able to answer reasonable questions from other Members and interested parties concerning the Member's proposed or existing measures and provides relevant documents, as appropriate. It also requires each WTO Member to ensure that all standards-related measures that it adopts are promptly published or otherwise made publicly available.

The TBT Agreement requires each WTO Member to provide other Members the opportunity to participate in the development of mandatory standards-related measures, which helps to ensure that standards-related measures do not become unnecessary obstacles to trade.[5] In particular, the TBT Agreement requires each Member to publish a notice in advance that it proposes to adopt a technical regulation or conformity assessment procedure.[6] It also requires each WTO Member to notify proposed technical regulations and conformity assessment procedures to the WTO so that other WTO Members may comment on them in writing. WTO Members are required, without discrimination, to take into account these written comments, plus the results of any requested discussions of those comments, when finalizing their measures.[7] In 2012 alone, WTO Members notified 1,550 new or revised technical regulations and conformity assessment

---

[5] Depending on the WTO Member's domestic processes, interested parties may participate directly in that Member's process for developing new standards-related measures, for example, by submitting written comments to the Member, or indirectly by working with their own governments to submit comments.

[6] WTO Members typically do this by publishing a notice in an official journal of national circulation or on a government website that they propose to adopt a technical regulation or conformity assessment procedure or by publishing the full text of the draft measure.

[7] The obligations described in this paragraph apply to measures that have a significant effect on trade and are not based on relevant international standards, guides, or recommendations or in circumstances where relevant international standards, guides, or recommendations do not exist. In many instances, however, Members, including the United States, notify proposed technical regulations and conformity assessment procedures regardless of whether they are based on relevant international standards.

procedures, as well as submitted 575 addenda and 45 corrigenda to previous notifications. Since entry into force of the Marrakesh Agreement Establishing the World Trade Organization (WTO Agreement)[8] on January 1, 1995, up to December 31, 2012, 15,736 notifications along with 2,684 addenda and 485 corrigenda to these notifications have been made by 116 members. Box 3 shows the number of notifications yearly since 1995.[9]

Box 3. *Number of TBT Notifications since 1995*[10]

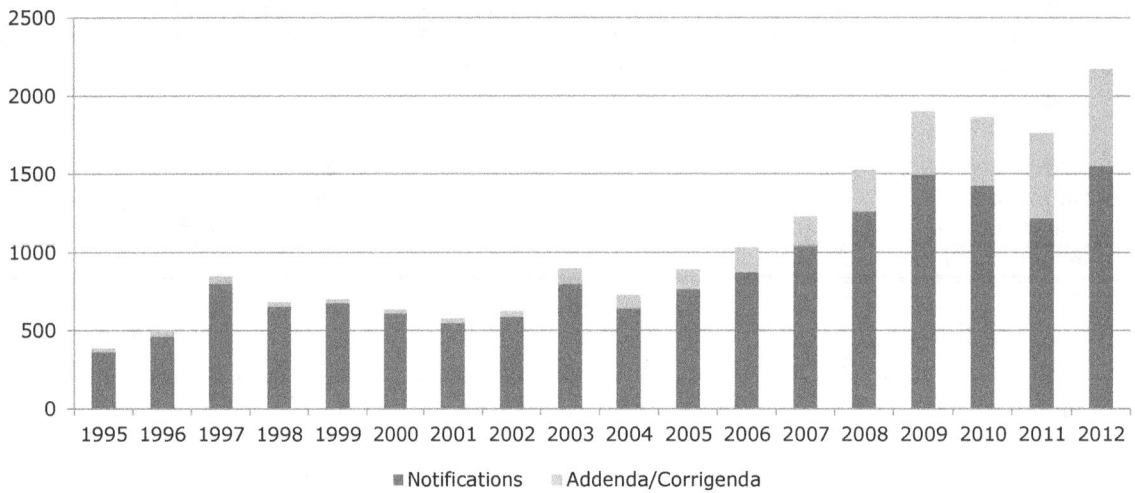

Article 13 of the TBT Agreement establishes a "Committee on Technical Barriers to Trade" to oversee the operation and implementation of the TBT Agreement. The TBT Committee is open to participation by all 159 WTO Members. The TBT Committee is one of over a dozen standing bodies (others include the Committees on Import Licensing, Antidumping Practices, and Rules of Origin, for example) that report to the WTO Council for Trade in Goods. The activities of the TBT Committee are described in detail below.

Operation of the TBT Agreement

The TBT Agreement sets out rules covering complex requirements developed and implemented by disparate bodies (central and local governmental agencies; inter-governmental entities; and non-governmental, national, and international standardizing organizations). WTO Members' central government authorities have primary responsibility for ensuring compliance with the TBT Agreement, including by taking reasonable measures to ensure that local and non-governmental bodies, such as private sector standards developing organizations, comply with

---

[8] The TBT Agreement is one of several agreements, understandings and decisions comprising the WTO Agreement.

[9] WTO Members notify new measures, as well as addenda and corrigenda to previously notified measures. An addendum alerts WTO Members that substantive or technical changes have been made to a measure that has been previously notified. A corrigendum conveys editorial or administrative corrections to a previous notification. Many Members also notify adopted technical regulations and conformity assessment procedures (regardless of whether or not they are based on relevant international standards).

[10] Number of TBT Notifications since 1995 found in "Eighteenth Annual Review of the Implementation and Operation of the TBT Agreement (G/TBT/33)."

the relevant provisions. Further, each WTO Member must inform the TBT Committee of the laws, policies, and procedures it has adopted to implement and administer the TBT Agreement.[11]

The quality and coherence of these laws, policies, and procedures – as well as how they are put into practice – influence the extent to which standards-related measures in any particular country are transparent, non-discriminatory, and avoid creating unnecessary obstacles to trade, as the TBT Agreement requires. Sound mechanisms for internal coordination among a WTO Member's trade, regulatory, and standards officials are critical to ensuring that the Member effectively implements the TBT Agreement. When interested agencies and officials coordinate their efforts in developing standards-related measures, it makes it more likely that the government will consider alternative technical specifications that may reduce any adverse effects on trade while still fulfilling the measure's objective.

Further, when governments take account of how the products they propose to regulate are traded in foreign markets, it can actually make the measures they adopt more effective in fulfilling their objectives. The effectiveness of a WTO Member's internal coordination also often determines the extent to which it is able to resolve specific trade concerns raised by other Members. Accordingly, in some developing countries, ineffective internal coordination and a lack of established procedures for developing standards-related measures are a key concern. For these countries, technical assistance or cooperative efforts to improve internal coordination can be vital in helping U.S. exporters sell into these markets.

The TBT Committee conducts triennial reviews of systemic issues affecting WTO Members' policies and procedures for implementing specific obligations.[12] In the course of these reviews, Members adopt specific recommendations and decisions, and lay out a forward-looking work program to strengthen the implementation and operation of the TBT Agreement. To advance their understanding of systemic issues, Members share experiences and participate in special events and regional workshops to explore topics in depth. In recent years, Committee events have covered good regulatory practice, conformity assessment, transparency, the role of international standards in development, and regulatory cooperation.

In addition to its triennial reviews and the related special events and workshops, the TBT Committee also meets three times a year. At these meetings, Members may raise any specific trade concern regarding standards-related measures that other WTO Members have proposed or adopted. The Committee's discussion of these concerns can help to clarify the technical aspects of the measures concerned, promote greater understanding of how the measures might affect trade, and perhaps even help to resolve the concerns. In 2012, WTO Members raised over 94 specific trade concerns in the TBT Committee, including, for example, concerns regarding measures relating to managing hazards arising from use of chemicals, labeling and other non-safety requirements relating to food products, and duplicative or redundant testing requirements on a wide variety of goods such as toys and medical devices. WTO Members have underscored

---

[11] See G/TBT/GEN/1/Rev.11 for a list of Members' submissions on the measures they have taken to implement and administer the TBT Agreement.

[12] The Committee's work on the outcome of the most recent triennial review is discussed in Section IX.

the importance of the Committee's regular discussions of specific trade concerns, and agreed that the Committee's work has helped to clarify and resolve trade issues between WTO Members.[13]

Box 4 shows the number of specific trade concerns WTO Members have raised in the TBT Committee since 1995. The general increase in concerns raised over the past few years reflects several factors – including an increase in the number of proposed measures that WTO Members have notified to the WTO, a heightened focus on standards-related activities, increased concern that these measures may be used as a form of disguised protectionism, and an increasing perception that discussions in the TBT Committee, as well as bilateral discussions on the margins of Committee meetings, can lead to results in addressing trade concerns. For a full accounting of the concerns raised in the Committee since 1995, see G/TBT/31.

Box 4. *Number of specific trade concerns raised per year*[14]

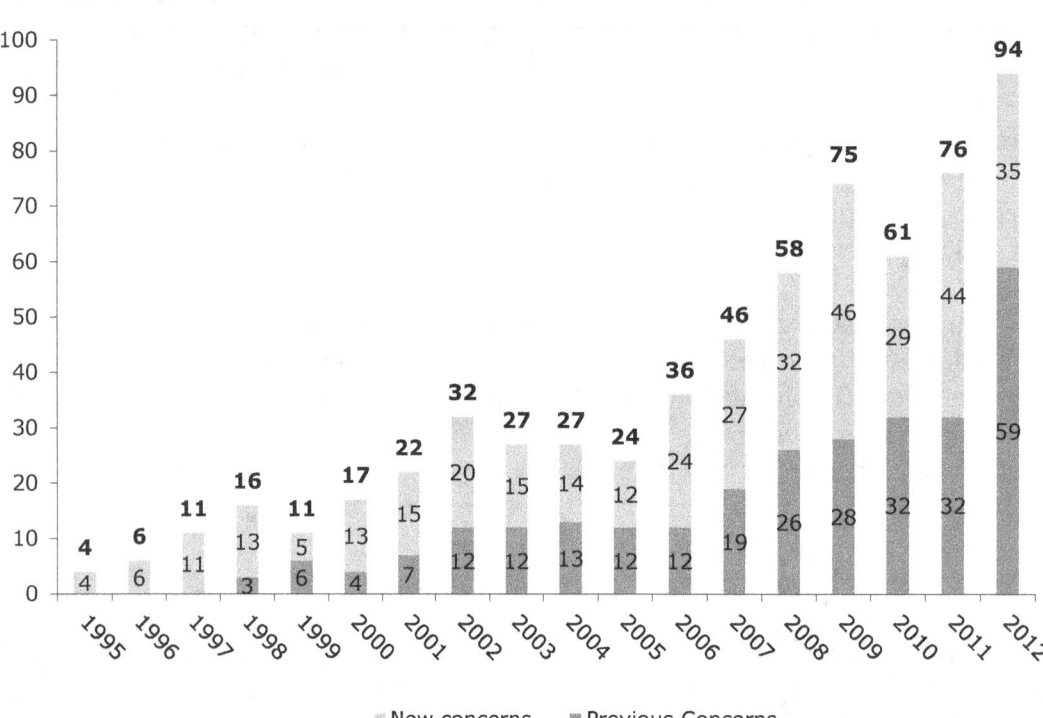

In recent years, the Committee has implemented procedures to streamline the discussion of specific trade concerns during its meetings and avoid unnecessary repetition. While addressing specific trade concerns is core to the Committee's responsibility in monitoring how well WTO Members are implementing the TBT Agreement, some exchanges on unresolved issues have become protracted, leaving less time for the Committee to address the cross-cutting or systemic

---

[13] See the discussion of the Operation of the Committee in the *"Fifth Triennial Review of the Operation and Implementation of the Agreement on Technical Barriers to Trade under Article 15.4"* G/TBT/26.

[14] Number of specific trade concerns raised since 1995, found in "Eighteenth Annual Review of the Implementation and Operation of the TBT Agreement (G/TBT/33)."

issues needed to prevent and resolve trade issues. In 2012, the Committee agreed to use informal "thematic" discussions on the margins of its meetings in 2013, in order to sharpen focus and make progress on key systemic issues. In 2013, the Committee held thematic discussions on standards and good regulatory practices in March and will hold thematic discussions on Transparency and Inquiry Point operations in June and conformity assessment in November.

Standards-Related Provisions in U.S. Free Trade Agreements

In U.S. FTAs, the parties reaffirm their commitment to the TBT Agreement. U.S. FTAs build on the disciplines in the TBT Agreement in important ways, including by providing for greater transparency, establishing mechanisms for more in-depth consultation on specific trade concerns, and facilitating cooperation and coordination with FTA partners on systemic issues. As a result, the U.S. approach to standards-related measures in its FTAs is commonly referred to as "TBT plus."[15] For example, recent FTAs require each party to allow persons of the other Party to participate in the development of standards, technical regulations and conformity assessment procedures. Moreover, each party is required to permit persons of the other party to participate in the development of these measures on terms no less favorable than it accords its own persons.

U.S. FTAs also contain a variety of other substantive obligations that go beyond those in the TBT Agreement. For example, U.S. FTAs require FTA partners to accredit or otherwise recognize U.S. testing and certification bodies under no less favorable terms than FTA partners accord their own testing and certification bodies. Recent U.S. FTAs, as well as the earlier NAFTA, also build in mechanisms (such as special committees) for closer and more enduring engagement and cooperation on standards-related measures. These mechanisms can prevent specific trade concerns from arising and assist the FTA governments in resolving emerging problems.

By enhancing understanding of each Party's respective rulemaking processes and standards and conformance processes, these consultative mechanisms can enable early identification of potential trade problems and provide opportunities for the FTA partners to discuss technical alternatives before a measure is finalized.[16] The provisions in U.S. FTAs that provide for more timely and robust consultations and participation, enhance the notifications process, and provide for direct bilateral engagement on notified measures are particularly important in this regard. These consultative mechanisms can provide a channel for peer-to-peer capacity building activities with FTA partners whose standards and conformance processes may be underdeveloped or otherwise in need of improvement.

Like the TBT Agreement, the TBT provisions of U.S. FTAs recognize that FTA partners should

---

[15] For a discussion of agreements that promote divergence from multilateral approaches (or "TBT minus") see Trade Policy Working Paper No. 58, *Do Bilateral and Regional Approaches for Reducing Technical Barriers to Trade Converge Towards The Multilateral Trading System?* (OECD (TAD/TC/WP (2007)12/FINAL).

[16] See, for example, G/TBT/W/317 for a discussion of the cooperative standards-related work on automobiles, chemicals, food, energy, and other issues under the NAFTA.

not be prevented from taking measures necessary to protect public health and safety or the environment. At the same time, U.S. FTAs provide mechanisms through which FTA partners can reduce the negative effects on their bilateral trade stemming from unnecessary differences in their regulatory regimes. Several U.S. FTAs also contain provisions designed to encourage FTA partners to accept each other's regulations as equivalent to their own, where appropriate.

Lastly, recent U.S. FTAs provide strong support for the *U.S. Standards Strategy* – which establishes a framework for developing voluntary product standards – by formally recognizing the TBT Committee's *2000 Decision on Principles for the Development of International Standards*.[17] The U.S. experience with the *2000 Committee Decision* is described at length in G/TBT/W/305. These issues are discussed in more detail in Section VI below.

In 2012, the United States made significant progress with ten Asia Pacific trading partners through the Trans-Pacific Partnership (TPP) negotiations towards concluding a TBT chapter and several sectoral annexes addressing standards-related measures. Further details on the TPP are provided in Section IX below.

Box 5. Key Standards-Related Provisions in U.S. Free Trade Agreements

The United States has concluded FTAs with a number of countries. While each agreement is unique, many of these FTAs share common provisions relating to standards-related measures. This box summarizes standards-related provisions common to U.S. FTAs with Australia, Bahrain, Central America and the Dominican Republic, Chile, Colombia, Korea, Morocco, Oman, Panama, and Peru.

Affirmation of the TBT Agreement: The FTAs reaffirm the parties' obligations under the TBT Agreement and use the TBT Agreement's definitions of key terms, such as technical regulation, standard, and conformity assessment procedures.

International standards: The FTAs require FTA partners to apply the principles of the *2000 Committee Decision* in determining whether an international standard, guide, or recommendation exists.

Conformity assessment procedures: The FTAs recognize the variety of mechanisms that exist for facilitating acceptance of each other's conformity assessment procedures, and they list specific examples of those mechanisms. The agreements also call for FTA partners to intensify their exchange of information regarding these mechanisms; require an FTA partner to explain when it will not accept, or negotiate agreements to accept, another partner's conformity assessment results; call for FTA partners to recognize conformity assessment bodies in another partner's territory on a national treatment basis; and require FTA partners to explain any refusal to recognize another party's conformity assessment body.

Transparency: The FTAs expand upon transparency obligations provided for in the TBT Agreement. For example, US FTAs with Colombia, Peru and Korea provide that each party shall permit persons from the other party to participate in the development of standards-related measures on terms no less favorable than those it accords to its own persons and require parties (1) to notify proposed technical regulations even where those regulations are based on relevant international standards; (2) to notify proposals for technical regulations or conformity assessment procedures directly to the other Party; (3) to include in notifications of proposed technical regulations and conformity assessment procedures the objectives of the proposed measure and the proposed measure's rationale or how the measure meets those objectives; (4) to provide interested parties as well as the FTA partner a meaningful opportunity to comment on the proposed measure; (5) to allow at least 60 days for comment; (6) to provide responses to significant comments received no later than the time a final measure is published; and (7) to provide

---

[17] Decision on Principles for the Development of International Standards, Guides and Recommendations with Relation to Articles 2, 5 and Annex 3 of the TBT Agreement, contained in document G/TBT/1/Rev.10.

additional information about the objectives when requested.

Cooperation: The FTAs provide for FTA partners to intensify their joint work on technical regulations, standards, and conformity assessment procedures. They also urge parties to identify bilateral initiatives for specific issues or sectors.

Information Exchange: The FTAs call on each FTA partner to provide information or explanations regarding proposed measures within a reasonable period following a request from another FTA partner.

Administration: Each FTA creates its own committee or subcommittee to monitor application of the agreement's provisions, address specific issues that arise under the agreement, enhance cooperation, and exchange information on pertinent developments.

Note: For more information, see http://www.ustr.gov/trade-agreements/free-trade-agreements.

V. U.S. Statutory and Administrative Framework for Implementing Standards-Related Trade Obligations

The United States maintains a robust system to support implementation of its trade obligations on standards-related measures through strong central management of its regulatory regime, an effective interagency trade policy mechanism, and public consultation. The legal framework for implementing U.S. obligations under the TBT Agreement and standards-related provisions in U.S. FTAs includes the *Administrative Procedure Act of 1946* (APA) and the *Trade Agreements Act of 1979* (TAA).[18] The APA establishes a process of public participation in rulemakings by U.S. agencies through a system of notice and comment. The TAA prohibits Federal agencies from engaging in any standards-related activity that creates unnecessary obstacles to trade and directs them to consider the use of international standards in rulemaking.

The TAA establishes USTR as the lead agency within the Federal Government for coordinating and developing international trade policy regarding standards-related activities, as well as in discussions and negotiations with foreign governments on standards-related matters. In carrying out this responsibility, USTR is required to inform and consult with Federal agencies having expertise in the matters under discussion and negotiation. The TAA also directs the Secretaries of Commerce and Agriculture to keep abreast of international standards activities, to identify those activities that may substantially affect U.S. commerce, and to inform, consult, and coordinate with USTR with respect to international standards-related activities.

The APA provides the foundation for transparency and accountability in developing Federal regulations. The APA requires agencies to undertake a notice and comment process open to all members of the public, both foreign and domestic, for all rulemakings, and to take these comments into account in the final rule.[19] In accordance with the APA, agencies publish proposed technical regulations and conformity assessment procedures in the *Federal Register* and solicit comments from the public through notices published in the *Federal Register*. To fulfill WTO obligations to notify proposed technical regulations and conformity assessment procedures, the National Institute of Standards and Technology (NIST) in the Department of Commerce serves as the U.S. notification authority and inquiry point for purposes of the TBT Agreement. The U.S. inquiry point reviews the *Federal Register* and other materials on a daily basis and notifies the WTO of technical regulations and conformity assessment procedures that agencies propose to adopt.

---

[18] The standards-related provisions of the TAA are codified at United States Code, Title 19, Chapter 13, Subchapter II, Technical Barriers to Trade (Standards).

[19] The term "rule" refers to "an agency statement of general or particular applicability and future effect designed to implement, interpret, or prescribe law or policy...." 5 U.S.C. § 551(4). "Rule making" means the "agency process for formulating, amending, or repealing a rule...." 5 U.S.C. § 551(5). These definitions include rules or rulemakings regarding technical regulations and conformity assessment procedures. The APA makes exceptions for urgent matters, allowing Federal agencies to omit notice and comment, for example, where they find that notice and public procedures are impracticable or contrary to the public interest. 5 U.S.C. § 553(b)(3).

The foundation for central regulatory review is *Executive Order 12866 – Regulatory Planning and Review* (E.O. 12866) and the implementing guidance of the Office and Management and Budget (OMB) *Circular A-4*. E.O. 12866 lays out the regulatory philosophy, principles, and actions that guide federal agencies in planning, developing, and reviewing Federal regulations. E.O. 12866 and Circular A-4 are the primary basis on which good regulatory practice (GRP) has been integrated into the Federal regulatory structure. These practices ensure openness, transparency, and accountability in the regulatory process, and, as a result, help ensure that the United States fulfills key TBT Agreement and U.S. FTA obligations. GRP,[20] such as that embodied in E.O. 12866 and Circular A-4, enables government agencies to achieve their public policy objectives efficiently and effectively. GRP is also critical in reducing the possibility that governments will adopt standards-related measures that create unnecessary obstacles to trade.

Under the procedures set out in E.O. 12866, prior to adopting any significant regulatory action (*e.g.*, a proposed technical regulation) Federal agencies must submit it for review to OMB. Significant regulatory actions are defined as those with an estimated annual impact on the U.S. economy of at least $100 million. OMB reviews Federal agencies' proposed regulatory actions and consults with USTR and other agencies as needed. This review is designed to ensure, *inter alia*, that proposed regulatory actions are not duplicative or inconsistent with other planned or existing Federal regulatory actions, are consistent with U.S. international trade obligations, and take into account the trade impact of proposed regulatory actions. At the conclusion of this process, OMB provides guidance to the pertinent agency to ensure that its regulatory actions are consistent with applicable law, Presidential priorities, and E.O. 12866's regulatory principles.

On January 18, 2011, President Obama issued *Executive Order 13563 - Improving Regulation and Regulatory Review* (E.O. 13563), which reaffirms and supplements E.O. 12866. E.O. 13563 states that "[the U.S.] regulatory system must protect public health, welfare, safety, and our environment while promoting economic growth, innovation, competitiveness, and job creation . . . . It must allow for public participation and an open exchange of ideas. It must promote predictability and reduce uncertainty. It must identify and use the best, most innovative and least burdensome tools for achieving regulatory ends. It must take into account benefits and costs, both quantitative and qualitative." E.O. 13563 sets out certain regulatory principles, as well as new requirements designed to promote public participation, improve regulatory integration and innovation, increase flexibility, ensure scientific integrity, and increase retrospective analysis of existing rules.

---

[20] For a discussion of good regulatory practices from the perspective of APEC and the OECD, see:

APEC, "*Information Notes on Good Practice for Technical Regulation*," September 2000.

OECD, *Cutting Red Tape: National Strategies for Administrative Simplification*. Paris, 2006.

OECD, *Background Document on Oversight Bodies for Regulatory Reform*. Paris: OECD, 2007.

OECD, *Regulatory Impact Analyses: Best Practices in OECD Countries*. Paris: OECD, 1997.

OECD, *Regulatory Performance: Ex post Evaluation of Regulatory Policies*. Paris: OECD, 2003.

OECD and APEC, *APEC-OECD Integrated Checklist on Regulatory Reform*. Mexico City, 2005.

On May 12, 2012, President Obama issued *Executive Order 13610 - Identifying and Reducing Regulatory Burdens* (E.O. 13610), which requires agencies to conduct retrospective analyses of existing rules to examine whether they remain justified and whether they should be modified or streamlined in light of changed circumstances, including the emergence of new technologies.

In addition to the statutes and policies outlined above, the *National Technology Transfer and Advancement Act* (NTTAA) and OMB's implementing guidance to Federal agencies, *OMB Circular A-119*, require Federal agencies to use[21] voluntary consensus standards[22] in their regulatory activities wherever possible and to avoid using "government-unique" standards.[23] The purpose is to discourage Federal agencies from developing their own standards where suitable voluntary consensus standards already exist. OMB will revise A-119, and will seek comments from the public on the changes in 2013.

Voluntary consensus standards can often effectively achieve an agency's regulatory objectives. The NTTAA and the TAA are complementary: the NTTAA directs Federal agencies to look to voluntary consensus standards to meet their regulatory objectives, while the TAA directs them to consider using relevant international standards. As elaborated in Section VI, international standards are those that recognized bodies, either intergovernmental or non-governmental, develop in accordance with principles such as openness, transparency, and consensus.

For additional information on the laws, policies, and interagency processes through which the United States implements the TBT Agreement, see G/TBT/2/Add.2, G/TBT/W/285, and G/TBT/W/315. See also the *Report on the Use of Voluntary Standards in Support of Regulation in the United States* presented to the High Level Regulatory Cooperation Forum of the United States – European Union Transatlantic Economic Council (TEC) in October 2009. For additional information on the relationship between technical barriers to trade and GRP, see G/TBT/W/287 and USITC Working Paper No ID-24, *The Role of Good Regulatory Practice in Reducing Technical Barriers to Trade*. In 2012, APEC published two related studies. The first study, "Good Regulatory Practices in APEC Member Economies - Baseline Study," reviews the application of selected GRPs across the 21 APEC members. The report focuses on several procedures that promote good regulatory practices particularly important to trade and investment such as accountability, consultation, efficiency, and transparency. The second study, "*Supporting the TBT Agreement with Good Regulatory Practices*," explores the relationship between TBT obligations and current GRPs used around the world. These recommended GRPs demonstrate choices available to WTO Members for implementation of practices that support trade-friendly regulation and implementation of their WTO commitments.

---

[21] Circular A-119 defines "use" as the inclusion of a standard in whole, in part, or by reference in a regulation.

[22] Circular A-119 states that the following attributes define bodies that develop voluntary consensus standards: openness, balance of interests, due process, an appeals process, and consensus.

[23] Circular A-119 defines "government-unique standards" as standards developed by the government for its own uses.

VI. Standards

Voluntary standards serve a variety of functions and their use supports world trade, for example, by promoting the connectivity and compatibility of inputs sourced in global markets. The TBT Agreement defines "standard" as:

> a document approved by a recognized body that provides, for common and repeated use, rules, guidelines or characteristics for products or related processes and production methods for which compliance is not mandatory.

Voluntary standards can facilitate buyer-seller transactions, spur competition[24] and innovation, increase the efficiency of production, unify markets, and promote societal goals. When used as the basis for establishing a technical requirement in a regulation, voluntary standards can help officials harness relevant technology to achieve regulatory objectives in a cost effective manner. In the United States, responsibility for developing voluntary standards rests almost exclusively, and appropriately, with the private sector, as this is where the technical know-how for sophisticated products and complex processes resides.[25]

The TBT Agreement acknowledges the diversity of standardizing bodies, and seeks to minimize unnecessary obstacles to trade that can arise from multiple standards for the same product, specifications that favor domestic goods over imported ones, lack of transparency, or dominance by a region or government in standards development. To promote greater harmonization of the technical requirements that WTO Members impose, the TBT Agreement promotes the use of and participation in the development of international standards. The TBT Agreement also strongly discourages standardizing bodies from developing standards where international standards already exist.

Additionally, the TBT Agreement requires Members to base technical regulations and conformity assessment procedures on relevant international standards, guides and recommendations, except where they would be inappropriate or ineffective in meeting a legitimate objective. The TBT Agreement affords technical regulations based on relevant international standards a rebuttable presumption that they are not unnecessary obstacles to trade under the TBT Agreement.

The TBT Agreement does not, however, designate specific standardizing bodies as "international." Instead, in its *2000 Decision on the Principles for the Development of International Standards, Guides and Recommendations (2000 Committee Decision)*, the TBT Committee adopted a set of six principles for developing international standards.[26] The *2000*

---

[24] See *Standards & Competitiveness: Coordinating for Results: Removing Standards-Related Trade Barriers Through Effective Collaboration*, International Trade Administration, 2005, available at http://www.trade.gov/td/standards/pdf%20files/Standards%20and%20Competitiveness.pdf.

[25] Agriculture is a notable exception. USDA maintains several programs, such as the Agricultural Marketing Service, for the development of voluntary standards on the quality and identity of agricultural products sold in the U.S. market.

[26] Decision on Principles for the Development of International Standards, Guides and Recommendations with

Committee Decision is designed to clarify the concept of "international standard" and to advance objectives such as greater harmonization of technical requirements across markets. The six principles are: (1) openness; (2) transparency; (3) impartiality and consensus; (4) relevance and effectiveness; (5) coherence; and (6) the development dimension.

It is the policy of the U.S. Government to use the term "international standard" to refer to those standards developed in conformity with the *2000 Committee Decision* principles.[27] For example, U.S. FTAs require trading partners to apply the *2000 Committee Decision* principles when determining whether a relevant international standard exists. When WTO Members use international standards developed in conformity with the *2000 Committee Decision* in their technical regulations, it can promote greater global regulatory alignment and reduce the adverse trade effects that regulatory divergences can create. Application of principles such as consensus, openness, and transparency when developing standards helps ensure standards are globally relevant and respond to both technical and regulatory needs. The *2000 Committee Decision* also helps ensure that all interested parties, including producers and consumers that may be affected by a particular standard, can participate in developing it.

Annex 3 of the TBT Agreement contains a *Code of Good Practice* for WTO Members and non-governmental standardizing bodies to follow in preparing, adopting, and applying standards. Central government standardizing bodies must adhere to the *Code*.[28] WTO Members' central government standardizing bodies are required to comply with the *Code*, and WTO Members are required to take reasonable measures to ensure that local government bodies and non-governmental standardizing bodies conform to the *Code* as well. In the United States, the American National Standards Institute (ANSI) has accepted the *Code of Good Practice* on behalf of the over 200 standards developing organizations (SDOs) that ANSI has accredited. ANSI, a private sector body, is the coordinator of the U.S. voluntary standards system with a membership that consists of standards developers, certification bodies, industry, government, and other stakeholders. In coordination with its membership, ANSI developed and implements the *U.S. Standards Strategy*.[29] For more information on the ANSI system, see *Overview of the U.S. Standardization System*.

ANSI accredits SDOs based on its *Essential Requirements*. Many elements of these requirements mirror the principles contained in the *2000 Committee Decision*. The *Essential Requirements* require each SDO to maintain procedures for developing standards that ensure openness, consensus, due process, and participation by materially affected interests. ANSI also serves as the U.S. national standards body member of the International Organization for Standardization (ISO) and the International Electrotechnical Commission (IEC). Federal agency representatives participate actively in ANSI policy forums, as well as in the technical committees of ANSI-accredited SDOs, on an equal basis as other ANSI members.

Relation to Articles 2, 5 and Annex 3 of the TBT Agreement are contained in document G/TBT/1/Rev.10.

[27] The U.S. experience with the *2000 Committee Decision* is described in G/TBT/W/305.

[28] Available at http://www.wto.org/english/docs_e/legal_e/17-tbt_e.htm

[29] Available at http://www.ansi.org/standards_activities/nss/usss.aspx.

OMB Circular A-119 contains guidance for Federal agencies in participating in the development of voluntary standards.[30] *Circular A-119* directs Federal agencies to use voluntary consensus standards in lieu of government-unique standards except where inconsistent with law or otherwise impractical. The Circular also provides guidance for Federal agencies participating in voluntary consensus standards bodies. The Interagency Committee for Standards Policy, which NIST chairs, coordinates implementation of this guidance. More than 4,000 Federal agency officials participate in the private sector standards development activities of 497 organizations[31] to support regulatory needs, enable efficient procurement, and to help devise solutions to support emerging national priorities. It is notable, however, that the governments in some regions and countries take a non-technical and more commanding role in standards setting than Federal agencies generally do. For example, some governments direct their national standards bodies or central government bodies to develop voluntary standards to achieve specific regulatory needs.

---

[30] Available at http://www.whitehouse.gov/omb/circulars_a119/.

[31] Source: NIST, 2008.

VII. Conformity Assessment Procedures

The TBT Agreement defines "conformity assessment procedures" as: "Any procedure used, directly or indirectly, to determine that relevant requirements in technical regulations or standards are fulfilled." Outside the TBT Agreement, conformity assessment procedures may also encompass a broader set of procedures, for example, good manufacturing practices that are not related to product characteristics.

Conformity assessment enables buyers, sellers, consumers, and regulators to have confidence that products sourced in domestic and foreign markets meet specific requirements.[32] Governments may mandate conformity assessment procedures – such as testing, sampling, and certification requirements – to ensure that the requirements they have established in standards or regulations for a product, process, system, person, or body are fulfilled. Suppliers also use conformity assessment procedures to demonstrate to their customers that their products or related processes or systems meet particular specifications.[33]

Yet, the costs and delays attributable to unnecessary, duplicative, and unclear conformity assessment requirements are frequently cited as a key concern for U.S. exporters.[34] Indeed, many specific trade concerns that the United States has raised in the TBT Committee with respect to other WTO Members' measures center on difficulties associated with the Member's conformity assessment requirements. Governments can reduce or minimize such difficulties by taking into account the risks associated with a product's failure to conform to an underlying standard or requirement when choosing the type of conformity assessment procedure to apply with respect to that standard or requirement. Governments can also reduce or minimize costs associated with conformity assessment by adopting approaches that facilitate the acceptance of the results of those procedures (*e.g.*, approaches that allow products to be tested or certified in the country of export). The TBT Committee's list of approaches that facilitate this acceptance is contained in G/TBT/1/Rev.10.

In the United States, the NTTAA directs NIST to coordinate the conformity assessment activities of Federal, state, and local entities with private sector technical standards activities and conformity assessment activities. The goal is to eliminate any unnecessary duplication of these activities. Pursuant to this statutory directive, NIST published a notice in the *Federal Register*

---

[32] Conformity assessment procedures take a variety of forms, including, for example, testing, certification, registration, inspection, accreditation, and verification. The entities that conduct these procedures are referred to as conformity assessment bodies and include such bodies as testing laboratories, certification bodies, and accreditation bodies. Testing laboratories, for example, test products to evaluate their performance or product characteristics while certification bodies certify that products conform to specific standards or requirements. Accreditation bodies, for example, evaluate the competency of testing and certification bodies and verify that they comply with specific standards or requirements.

[33] For an introduction to conformity assessment, see Breitenberg, Maureen, *The ABC's of the U.S. Conformity Assessment System*, NIST, 1997.

[34] See Johnson, Christopher, *Technical Barriers to Trade: Reducing the Impact of Conformity Assessment Measures*, U.S. International Trade Commission Working Paper, 2008.

in 2000 providing guidance to Federal agencies on conformity assessment.[35] This notice calls for Federal agencies to provide sound rationales, seek public comments, look to the results of other government and private sector organizations, and use international guides and standards when incorporating conformity assessment procedures in their regulations and procurement processes. Today, the conformity assessment standards and guides published by ISO and IEC are known as the "CASCO toolbox."[36]

In addition to NIST's efforts to inform and guide Federal agencies in adopting and applying conformity assessment procedures, Federal agencies and private sector organizations can look to guidance in ANSI's *National Conformity Assessment Principles for the United States*.[37] The TBT Agreement, NIST's guidance, and ANSI's principles all emphasize the importance of the development and use of international conformity assessment standards and participation in international accreditation systems in facilitating international trade.

Participation and use of international systems of conformity assessment strengthens these international systems and produces global benefits. For example, international systems for accreditation play a vital role in allowing products to be tested and certified at sites that are convenient to production facilities and reducing duplicative testing and certification requirements. International systems for accreditation enable this by establishing procedures and criteria that accreditation bodies participating in the system agree to apply when accrediting testing, certification, or other conformity assessment bodies. Accreditations issued by such entities can, in appropriate circumstances, provide governments, as well as suppliers, assurances that a body – regardless of its location – is competent to test and certify products for relevant markets.

Examples of international accreditation systems include the International Laboratory Accreditation Cooperation (ILAC) and the International Accreditation Forum (IAF). ILAC and IAF have established voluntary mutual recognition arrangements (MRAs). Under these MRAs, accreditation bodies agree to adhere to international standards and other procedures and criteria when accrediting testing and certification bodies and subject themselves to a system of peer-to-peer review to ensure that they continue to meet MRA requirements. U.S. accreditation bodies that participate in these mutual recognition arrangements are predominately private sector entities. Increasingly, Federal agencies, such as the Consumer Product Safety Commission and the Nuclear Regulatory Commission, are using international systems such as ILAC in support of their conformity assessment requirements.

---

[35] http://gsi.nist.gov/global/docs/FR_FedGuidanceCA.pdf

[36] ISO/CASCO is the standards development and policy committee on conformity assessment of ISO.

[37] http://publicaa.ansi.org/sites/apdl/Documents/News%20and%20Publications/Brochures/NCAP%20second%20edition.pdf

VIII. U.S. Processes for Identifying Standards-Related Trade Barriers and Determining How to Address Them

The United States maintains rigorous, interagency processes and mechanisms for identifying, reviewing, analyzing, and addressing foreign government standards-related measures that act, or may act, as barriers to U.S. trade. USTR coordinates these processes and mechanisms through the TPSC and, more specifically, its specialized TBT subgroup, the TPSC Subcommittee on Technical Barriers to Trade (TPSC Subcommittee).

The TPSC Subcommittee, comprising representatives from Federal regulatory agencies and other agencies with an interest in foreign standards-related measures, meets formally at least three times a year, but maintains an ongoing process of informal consultation and coordination on standards-related issues as they arise. Representatives of the Subcommittee include officials from the Departments of Agriculture, Commerce, and State – as well as officials from OMB and Federal regulatory agencies, such as the Food and Drug Administration and the Environmental Protection Agency. The Departments of Commerce and Agriculture serve as the primary conduits for communicating information between U.S. industry and agriculture export interests, respectively, and the TPSC Subcommittee.

Information for the TPSC Subcommittee on foreign standards-related measures is collected and evaluated on a day-to-day basis through a variety of government channels including: the U.S. TBT Inquiry Point and Notification Authority (U.S. TBT Inquiry Point) at NIST, the Trade Compliance Center (TCC), the Office of Standards Liaison, and the U.S. Commercial Service (UCS) in the Department of Commerce; the Foreign Agricultural Service (FAS) and its Office of Agreements and Scientific Affairs (OASA) in the Department of Agriculture; the State Department's economic officers in U.S embassies abroad; and USTR. U.S. Government outreach and consultations with U.S. stakeholders generates much of the information supplied through these channels, which are further described below.

To disseminate information to U.S. stakeholders on proposed foreign notifications of standards-related measures, the U.S. Inquiry Point operates a web-based service, *Notify U.S.*, which automatically notifies registered stakeholders of measures proposed and adopted by other WTO Members in sectors of interest.[38] These notifications alert U.S. firms and other interested stakeholders of their opportunity to comment on proposed foreign measures that may have an impact on their exports. U.S. stakeholders may provide their comments directly to the WTO Member concerned, if its domestic processes so provide, or through the U.S. Inquiry Point, which works with relevant Federal agencies to review, compile and submit comments to the WTO Member. By providing comments through the U.S. Inquiry Point, U.S. stakeholders alert Federal agencies to their concerns and enable advocacy by Federal agencies on their behalf.

In 2012, the U.S. TBT Inquiry Point distributed 2,176 WTO TBT notifications to registered stakeholders, including 248 U.S. notifications. The U.S. TBT Inquiry Point processed 450 requests for information on standards and technical regulations and fulfilled 728 requests for full-text documents associated with TBT notifications. The U.S. TBT Inquiry Point distributed

---
[38] Available at https://tsapps.nist.gov/notifyus/data/index/index.cfm

190 U.S. Government and industry comments to other WTO Members and circulated 26 WTO Member comments on U.S. measures, as well as 27 WTO Member replies to U.S. comments, to relevant Federal agencies. U.S. stakeholders monitor notifications of new or revised measures of other WTO Members in sectors of interest through *Notify U.S.* (which added more than 400 new subscribers in 2012), and contact U.S. officials through the government channels listed above to obtain further information, to contribute to the submission of U.S. comments, and to coordinate follow-up actions. The U.S TBT Inquiry Point hosted or participated in training for eight U.S. and foreign visiting delegations interested in learning how a WTO inquiry point operates.

Through the Trade Agreements Compliance (TAC) Program, the U.S. Department of Commerce supports the enforcement prong of the National Export Initiative (NEI) by coordinating efforts and resources within the Department to systematically monitor, investigate, and help ensure foreign governments' compliance with trade agreements to which the United States is a party. The TAC Program includes an online trade complaint hotline at www.export.gov/tcc, where exporters can report and obtain assistance in overcoming foreign trade barriers. As part of the TAC Program, the Department of Commerce assembles teams of specialists to investigate market access problems, including those involving standards-related measures, as well as to develop strategies to address them. Compliance teams work with affected companies or industries to establish objectives and to craft and implement compliance action plans to achieve or improve market access.

In addition, the Department of Commerce regularly provides input to the TPSC and TPSC Subcommittee based on the information on the specific trade concerns that it collects and analyzes through the TAC Program. This informs the TPSC's development of the appropriate U.S. position in the various multilateral and bilateral forums for addressing standards-related measures. Compliance officers also provide on-the-ground assistance at U.S. embassies in China, India, El Salvador, and at the U.S. Mission to the European Union in Brussels. Free, online tools include the texts of more than 250 non-agricultural trade agreements plus a checklist of the kinds of trade barriers that the TAC Program can help exporters overcome.

The Department of Agriculture's OASA provides a conduit for queries and comments on foreign standards-related measures in the agricultural sector. OASA monitors developments in relevant export markets, provides information on foreign standards-related measures through a range of publications, disseminates TBT notifications from foreign governments to interested parties, and provides translation services on key export market requirements. OASA works cooperatively with U.S. industry, as well as with technical specialists in its overseas offices and Federal regulatory agencies, to develop comments and positions on specific foreign standards-related measures. In addition, the Department of Agriculture's FAS overseas offices maintain country-specific reporting and alerts that highlight foreign commodity-specific import requirements. These officers assist with detained shipments and help to identify innovative solutions to keep trade flowing. FAS also participates in numerous relevant international organizations, such as Codex Alimentarius, to proactively address agriculture-related trade concerns arising from foreign standards-related measures.

In addition to these government channels, the TPSC Subcommittee receives information from the Industry and Agriculture Trade Advisory Committees (ITACs and ATACs, respectively). The ITACs and the ATACs help identify trade barriers and provide assessments regarding the practical realities that producers face in complying with technical regulations and conformity assessment procedures. USTR and Commerce officials meet at least quarterly with the ITAC on Standards and Technical Trade Barriers (ITAC 16), which is composed of cleared advisors from manufacturers, trade associations, standards developers, and conformity assessment bodies.[39] USTR also meets with other ITACs and advisory committees to receive advice on TBT issues affecting specific industry sectors, such as steel, chemicals, automobiles, processed foods, and textiles, or specific regulatory areas, such as labor and the environment.

In developing the U.S. position on any foreign standards-related measure, the TPSC Subcommittee takes into account how the United States regulates the same or similar products. Regulatory agency officials on the TBT TPSC Subcommittee also provide important information on the technical and scientific aspects of particular foreign standards-related measures, as well as insights on cooperative efforts through international organizations that may be relevant to the issue. The TPSC Subcommittee factors the views that regulatory agencies express into the positions that the United States takes in multilateral, regional, and bilateral trade discussions regarding standards-related measures. Particularly in the area of emerging technologies where standards-related activities are nascent, the technical, scientific, and policy advice that regulatory agencies provide is critical in formulating U.S. views.

Engagement in Voluntary Standards Activities

In the United States, standards development is led by the private sector and highly informed by market needs. However, in limited circumstances, in areas relevant to their agency objectives, Federal government agencies also actively engage or play a convening role in standards development. In January 2012, USTR, OIRA, and OSTP released a joint memorandum to agencies entitled "Principles for Federal Engagement in Standards Activities to Address National Priorities"[40] to clarify principles guiding Federal agencies' engagement in standards activities. The memorandum emphasizes the strengths of the U.S. standards model of private sector leadership but notes that where a national priority has been identified in statute, regulation, or Administration policy, active engagement or a convening role by the Federal Government may be needed to accelerate standards development and implementation to spur technological advances, promote market-based innovation, and encourage more competitive market outcomes. The memorandum establishes five "fundamental strategic objectives" for Federal Government engagement in standards activities:

- produce timely, effective standards and efficient conformity assessment schemes that are essential to addressing an identified need;

- achieve cost-efficient, timely, and effective solutions to legitimate regulatory, procurement, and policy objectives;

---

[39] See http://www.ustr.gov/Who_We_Are/List_of_USTR_Advisory_Committees.html.

[40] Available at http://www.whitehouse.gov/sites/default/files/omb/memoranda/2012/m-12-08.pdf.

- promote standards and standardization systems that promote and sustain innovation and foster competition;

- enhance U.S. growth and competitiveness and ensure non-discrimination, consistent with international obligations; and

- facilitate international trade and avoid the creation of unnecessary obstacles to trade.

IX. U.S. Engagement on Standards-Related Measures in International, Regional, and Bilateral Fora

Overview of U.S. Engagement on Standards-Related Measures

The United States pursues a broad agenda and active engagement with foreign governments to prevent unnecessary obstacles to trade and to resolve specific trade concerns arising from standards-related measures. As noted above, the TBT Committee is the principal multilateral forum for engagement on trade issues relating to standards-related measures. The mechanisms for cooperation on these measures in U.S. FTAs also play a vital role in facilitating U.S. efforts to prevent and resolve standards-related trade concerns. In addition, U.S. agencies seek to prevent potential standards-related trade barriers from emerging by engaging in multilateral, regional, and bilateral cooperative activities, information exchanges, technical assistance, and negotiations on specific agreements. These efforts are aimed at helping other governments design effective and well-conceived standards-related measures, with the goal of producing better regulatory outcomes and facilitating trade.

U.S. Government cooperative efforts and information exchanges with other countries can assist firms in complying with standards-related measures. As producers increase their participation in global supply chains, they need a better understanding of technical requirements of countries, including the United States, and strategies to meet those requirements consistently. Cooperative activities can also serve to prevent localized high-profile incidents of the type that can disrupt trade across all markets and damage both producer reputations and consumer confidence. Close coordination among trade, regulatory, and standards officials with highly specialized technical expertise is required in order to carry out cooperation and information exchange initiatives that successfully meet these objectives.

The United States provides bilateral technical assistance and capacity building to developing countries on standards-related activities through the U.S. Agency for International Development (USAID), the U.S. Trade and Development Agency (USTDA), the Commerce Department's Commercial Law Development Program (CLDP) and Market Development Cooperator Program (MDCP), and NIST's Standards in Trade Program. USDA's FAS also provides technical assistance on standards-related to food trade. These agencies have broader missions and generally provide standards-related capacity building assistance as a component of a specific project or mission.

To reduce the negative impact on trade from divergences in technical requirements across markets, the United States negotiates bilateral, regional, and multilateral mutual recognition agreements (MRAs) with U.S. trading partners. These agreements establish procedures for each party to accept the results of conformity assessment procedures for specified products carried out in the other party's territory or to accept the other government's technical specifications for those products as sufficient to meet its own requirements. MRAs with trading partners that have a regulatory approach compatible with that of the United States and a similar level of technical capacity can help facilitate trade in select sectors where trade flows are significant and technical requirements can be complex, such as in the telecommunication equipment sector.

NIST maintains a complete inventory of the government-to-government MRAs to which the United States is a party.[41] It also maintains a listing of the accreditation requirements for conformity assessment bodies under each of these MRAs and a list of conformity assessment bodies that NIST has designated pursuant to each MRA as competent to perform tests or certify products to ensure they conform to the other MRA party's technical requirements. (The Federal Communications Commission (FCC) website provides useful background information on U.S. MRAs in the telecommunications sector and examples of how they work.)[42]

The United States also seeks to reduce foreign technical barriers to trade by concluding equivalency arrangements with other governments. In 2009, the United States exchanged the first equivalency determination with Canada on organic agricultural products. On February 15, 2012, the United States signed a second organics equivalence arrangement with the European Union.

U.S. engagement on standards-related measures in various international and regional fora is detailed below. U.S. bilateral engagement with its trading partners on standards-related measures is detailed in individual Country Specific Reports in Section XI.

WTO TBT Committee and Related Engagement

As noted above, the U.S. Government actively seeks to prevent and eliminate unnecessary technical barriers to trade through the focused WTO Member-driven agenda of the WTO TBT Committee ("TBT Committee"). The Committee dedicates a significant portion of each of its three annual meetings to affording Members the opportunity to raise specific trade concerns on measures that other Members have proposed or adopted. WTO Members may also use Committee sessions to share experiences, case studies, or concerns relating to cross-cutting issues regarding how Members are implementing the TBT Agreement. The TBT Committee often holds workshops or other events on special topics alongside its formal meetings. On the margins of each meeting, Members engage in informal bilateral and plurilateral meetings to clarify and resolve specific trade concerns and to discuss how to resolve other issues of mutual interest.

Specific Trade Concerns

In 2012, the United States raised specific trade concerns regarding on average 20 to 30 foreign TBT measures at each TBT Committee meeting and in the informal meetings it held with individual or groups of WTO Members. The details and status of many of the specific trade concerns that the United States raised in, and on the margins of, the TBT Committee sessions are described in Section XI of this report. As elaborated in Section XI, U.S. interventions in the TBT Committee, and on its margins, have helped resolve a number of standards-related concerns affecting U.S. trade. The Committee's annual review of its activities is contained in G/TBT/29, which includes a thumbnail description of the specific trade concerns that WTO Members raised and identifies the Members that raised them.

---

[41] Available at http://gsi.nist.gov/global/index.cfm/L1-4/L2-16.

[42] Available at http://transition.fcc.gov/oet/ea/mra/.

Systemic Issues

The TBT Agreement calls for the TBT Committee to review the implementation and operation of the Agreement every three years. These triennial reviews provide an important opportunity for WTO Members to clarify particular provisions of the Agreement. Triennial reviews have resulted in a significant body of agreed recommendations and decisions, contained in G/TBT/1/Rev.10, which are intended to strengthen and improve the operation of the TBT Agreement. Each triennial review also results in a report on the systemic issues the Committee discussed, along with a work plan to explore ways in which WTO Members can more effectively implement their TBT obligations.

In November 2011, the TBT Committee initiated its *Sixth Triennial Review of the Operation and Implementation of the Agreement on Technical Barriers to Trade under Article 15.4.* In the review, which concluded in November 2012, the Committee agreed to exchanges of information on (1) voluntary mechanisms and related principles of Good Regulatory Practices to guide members in efficient and effective implementation of the TBT Agreement; (2) approaches to, recognition of, and use of international standards for conformity assessment; (3) implementation of the *Code of Good Practice* by local governments and non-governmental bodies; and (4) the six principles of international standards development set out in the *2000 Committee Decision*, with particular focus on the development dimension and transparency.

The United States also launched a new U.S.-sponsored assistance facility called the "Standards Alliance" to help build capacity among developing countries to implement the TBT Agreement. The new Standards Alliance will help developing countries strengthen implementation of the TBT Agreement, including by improving their notification practices, by improving domestic practices related to adopting relevant international standards, and in clarifying and streamlining their regulatory processes for products. This program aims to reduce the costs and bureaucratic hurdles U.S. exporters face in foreign markets, and increase the competitiveness of American products, particularly in developing markets.

From October 30 through November 1, 2012, the U.S. Inquiry Point, in partnership with its Brazilian partner INMETRO and Standards Council Canada, hosted the first ever Inquiry Point of the Americas conference in Rio de Janeiro. The conference, a product of the U.S.-Brazil Commercial Dialogue, brought together nearly 200 TBT experts from thirty Western Hemisphere countries and the WTO in a workshop to exchange best practices regarding implementing transparency provisions of the WTO TBT Agreement and working with the private sector to improve the use of this valuable tool.

Total Economic Engagement Program

The Department of Commerce's Total Economic Engagement (TEE) Program provides technical assistance and capacity building to advance a more collaborative and open process to foster greater regulatory harmonization and convergence. TEE works with foreign governments, trade associations, and standards setting bodies on key public-private partnerships.

For example, in 2012, the TEE program sought to improve market access for U.S. certification bodies in China's compulsory certification (or CCC mark) testing regime. Through this program the Commerce Department urged China's Certification and Accreditation

Administration (CNCA) and China's Quality Certification Centre (CQC) to increase transparency, foster more predictable administrative processes, and develop more appropriately designed verification procedures for China's CCC program in accord with China's WTO commitments.

With the Russian Federation's recent membership in the WTO, Russia offers U.S. producers and exporters a potentially significant export market for high-quality products. To assist Russia in meeting its WTO commitments, the Commerce TEE program is conducting a series of outreach events across the United States and Russia to raise awareness of the new trade opportunities that will be afforded to U.S. companies.

Asia Pacific Economic Cooperation

APEC is the Asia-Pacific region's premiere inter-governmental economic organization. Its core mission is to strengthen regional economic integration by addressing barriers to trade and investment. APEC's twenty-one member economies comprise nearly half the world's population and more than half of the global economy. These member economies account for 55 percent of global GDP, purchase 58 percent of U.S. goods exports, and comprise a market of 2.7 billion customers. In fact, seven of the top 15 trade partners of the United States are members of APEC. In 2012, APEC focused on four areas: trade and investment liberalization and regional economic integration; strengthening food security; establishing reliable supply chains; and intensive cooperation to foster innovative growth.

As part of these efforts, the United States furthered work to prevent and eliminate unnecessary technical barriers related to emerging green technologies, such as those related to commercial green buildings and Smart Grid technology.[43] Additionally, the United States encouraged APEC economies to adopt standards and conformity assessment procedures that promote greener growth through the alignment of energy efficiency standards and conformity assessment procedures for information and communication technology (ICT) products. The areas of focus for 2012 with respect to green technologies included regional economic integration, product safety, supply chain integrity, and environmental protection. These green technology efforts with respect to Smart Grid, green buildings, and solar and ICT technologies, are further elaborated below. The United States also worked with APEC to advance regulatory cooperation dialogues regarding food and wine. APEC economies further recognized the importance of good regulatory practices and addressing unnecessary technical barriers to trade by advancing regulatory convergence and coherence.

Good Regulatory Practices

In 2012, APEC economies also re-affirmed their 2011 commitment to strengthen implementation of good regulatory practices, including through capacity building. In 2013, the United States will advance Good Regulatory Practices by updating the 2011 APEC Baseline

---

[43] The U.S. Department of Energy defines Smart Grid as an electrical grid that uses information and communications technology to gather and act on information, such as information about the behaviors of suppliers and consumers, in an automated fashion to improve the efficiency, reliability, economics, and sustainability of the production and distribution of electricity.

Study on member practices, developing a self-funded study on good regulatory practices with respect to conformity assessment, and participating in the 7th APEC Conference on Good Regulatory Practice, to be held in Medan, Sumatra in June 2013.

Smart Grid

Building on the success of the intensive dialogue and suggested trade-related principles on Smart Grid interoperability standards developed through the 2011 APEC Regulatory Cooperation Advancement Mechanism (ARCAM), the United States conducted a second workshop for energy regulators, entitled, "Regulatory Approaches to Smart Grid Investment and Deployment," on the margins of the World Forum on Energy Regulation held on May 16-17, 2012, in Quebec City, Canada. The conference sought to facilitate collaboration and information sharing between key stakeholder groups involved in the development of Smart Grid interoperability standards. The workshop responds to the APEC Committee on Trade and Investment (CTI) call for APEC economies to "implement mechanisms for internal coordination within APEC member economies among regulatory authorities, standards developing bodies and trade officials to advance interoperability of Smart Grid requirements."

The workshop recommended that regulators and standardization bodies continue and enhance discussion of developments and experiences regarding implementation of Smart Grid programs.

Green Buildings

Green buildings provide opportunities for U.S. companies to export a wide range of "green" products in which they have a competitive advantage, such as products related to plumbing, lighting, flooring, HVAC systems, and fixtures. The world imported $70 billion in U.S. building products in 2009, with APEC economies accounting for fully 70 percent of this total ($50 billion).

In addition, greening the commercial building sector can also yield significant energy savings, given that the sector accounts for between 30 and 40 percent of energy usage in most industrialized economies. These energy savings contribute to meeting greenhouse gas emissions targets, and improve energy security.

To advance these objectives, the United States supported two APEC studies on the subject of green buildings. The first study addressed green building rating systems in APEC economies. The second study addressed the trade impact of life cycle analysis for flooring materials and plumbing fixtures.

APEC Support Fund (ASF) has awarded the U.S. Department of Commerce $830,000 to serve as the project sponsor of a new APEC multi-year project on the relationship between standards and conformity assessment and energy efficient performance in commercial buildings. The project consists of a series of interrelated workshops and data gathering, which will occur from 2013-2015. These workshops and data gathering activities will aim to build the capacity of APEC economies to implement green building measures that are consistent, transparent, and appropriate, thus avoid creating unnecessary obstacles to trade. In 2013, Peru and the United States are working together to organize a workshop on "Sharing Experiences in the Design and Implementation of Green Building Codes" (March 2013). For this workshop, the United States will present a study on the use of building codes and green codes in the Asia Pacific region. The other workshop topics in the series include: Building Information Modeling (BIM) (June 2013); best practices in the testing and rating of products in the building envelope; and mapping of building product testing requirements. The United States is working together with the ASEAN Consultative Committee on Standards and Quality (ACCSQ) on these workshops.

Solar Technologies

The United States plans to introduce a project on solar technology and Smart Grid integration in 2013-2014. The goal of this project is to identify common goals, best practices, and strategies among APEC member economies that can facilitate Smart Grid and solar technology deployment as well as trade.

Information and Communication Technologies

Following the first successful dialogue in APEC on Information and Communication Technology (ICT) Energy Efficiency Standards, the United States organized a second workshop on the same subject in Seoul, Korea on July 18, 2012. Building on agreed principles from the first workshop, participants discussed the adoption and application of the ECMA383/IEC62623 standard.[44]

In 2013, the United States will suggest that APEC form a limited term working group of regulators to facilitate transition of personal computer energy efficiency programs to the new international standard.

APEC Food Safety Cooperation Forum (FSCF) and Partnership Training Institute Network (PTIN)

Trade in food and agricultural products in the Asia Pacific is vital to U.S. interests, yet concerns about food safety in the region spiked in recent years following a series of high-profile food safety incidents. These prompted APEC economies to agree to strengthen food safety standards and practices in the region and encourage adherence to international science-based standards to facilitate trade in the region and enhance food safety. In response, the APEC Subcommittee on Standards and Conformance (SCSC) established the Food Safety Cooperation Forum (FSCF) in 2007 with the goal of improving food safety regulatory systems in APEC economies in line with WTO Members' rights and obligations under both the SPS and TBT Agreements. In 2008, APEC economies called for increased capacity building to improve technical competence and understanding of food safety management among stakeholders in the food supply chain through the public-private partnership initiative, the Partnership Training Institute Network (PTIN).

Since 2007, over $4 million of public and private sector funds have been contributed for FSCF and PTIN activities. The FSCF and PTIN have identified priority capacity building needs and delivered over 30 programs in key areas (supply chain management, food safety incident management, laboratory competency, risk analysis, food safety regulatory systems) since their inception.

---

[44] ECMA383/IEC 62623:2012 covers personal computing products. It applies to desktop and notebook computers. This standard specifies a test procedure to enable the measurement of the power and energy consumption.

In 2012, the U.S. convened experts from the public and private sectors to develop a strategy to improve laboratory capacity in the APEC region. Funding for two to three pilot projects may be available for 2013. This work builds on previous PTIN efforts on laboratory capacity building, including three U.S.-led training sessions in 2012 on laboratory practices. In addition, the PTIN developed a supply chain management training module, which is now freely available on the PTIN website.

APEC awarded the United States $1.8 million to serve as the project sponsor for an APEC multi-year project: Building Convergence in Food Safety Standards and Regulatory Systems for 2013-2015 encompassing priorities that include food safety standards and best practices for small- and medium-sized enterprise, incident management, laboratory capacity, food inspection based on risk analysis, and proficiency testing. FSCF and PTIN Steering Group meetings are scheduled to occur in April 2013 at the second APEC Senior Officials Meeting (SOM 2) in 2013 to address a first suite of activities relate to these priorities.

Lastly, the PTIN continued to work closely with the World Bank through the newly established Global Food Safety Partnership (GFSP), including developing a three-year plan of coordinated activities on food safety with the GFSP.

Wine Regulatory Forum

In 2008, the SCSC created a Wine Regulatory Forum (WRF) to promote trade-facilitating regulation of wine. Wine exports are critically important to several APEC economies, with their wine product export market totaling $3.6 billion in 2010. Following the success of the first-ever regional meeting of wine regulators and industry representatives in 2011, New Zealand hosted the second meeting of the APEC WRF. On November 5-6, 2012, the APEC Wine Regulators Forum meeting entitled, "Risk Management & Certification in Wine Trade: Public-Private Dialogue," was held in Auckland, New Zealand. This was a follow-up to the highly successful meeting in San Francisco, in September 2011. The key themes of the meeting were risk management and certification in the APEC wine trade. Participants exchanged views on the issues of wine as a low food safety risk product and multiple certification requirements. In 2013, the United States has proposed a multi-year project, which includes a pilot for electronic certificates for wine.

Global Food Safety Partnership

In 2012, the United States and the food industry contributed an initial $1 million in start-up funds to launch the World Bank GFSP. The objective of the GFSP is to improve food safety systems. The GFSP is undertaking a five-year program for training and capacity building in food safety. GFSP held a training program on food safety prerequisites and hazard analysis and critical control points (HACCP) in Beijing in June 2012 and will expand this program in 2013. A HACCP aquaculture module will be ready by April 2013. An assessment of laboratory capacity in the APEC economies is also under way. Other initial training programs will be supported by a $1.8 million APEC funding commitment for 2013-2015.

Trans-Pacific Partnership

In November 2009, President Obama announced that the United States would participate in negotiations to conclude a comprehensive Asia-Pacific trade agreement: The Trans-Pacific

Partnership (TPP) Agreement. Through the TPP, the United States seeks to advance U.S. trade and investment opportunities in the Asia-Pacific by negotiating an ambitious, 21st century regional trade agreement. The TPP negotiations began with an initial group of countries comprising: Australia, Brunei Darussalam, Chile, Malaysia, New Zealand, Peru, Singapore, the United States, and Vietnam. In October 2012, Canada and Mexico joined the negotiations and participated in the round of negotiations held in Auckland, New Zealand in December 2012.

On standards-related measures, the United States is emphasizing several key issues, including regulatory transparency, the use of GRPs, and the acceptance of the results of conformity assessment procedures carried out in TPP countries. The overall U.S. objective is to establish rules and disciplines for standards-related measures that reduce the likelihood that TPP countries will create or maintain standards-related measures that act as barriers to trade.

In 2012, the TPP Working Group on Technical Barriers to Trade (TBT) made substantial progress to advance negotiations of the TBT chapter, including several sector-specific annexes. The TBT chapter includes obligations that build upon the WTO TBT Agreement (referred to as "TBT plus"), including obligations on transparency, conformity assessment and international standards, and sets a framework for addressing trade concerns and for advancing cooperative activities on standards-related measures. These obligations seek to prevent and reduce unnecessary costs and barriers to trade in the region. The sector-specific annexes include obligations regarding the development and implementation of standards-related measures to address unnecessary barriers to trade in products in specific sectors, such as cosmetics, pharmaceuticals, medical devices, information and communications technology products, wine and spirits, and food formulas.

In 2013, the TBT Working Group will press to conclude the TBT chapter and its annexes.

Free Trade Agreement – TBT Committee Meetings

The inaugural meeting of the United States-Colombia Trade Promotion Agreement's Committee on Technical Barriers to Trade (TBT Committee) was held in Washington, DC, on October 23-24, 2012. The two governments discussed their respective systems as well as particular issues such as biologics, diesel emissions, baby clothing, food safety standards, appliances, and cosmetics. The Colombian delegation also visited NIST for training on Inquiry Point operations.

Other FTA TBT Chapter meetings that were held in 2012 included the TBT Chapter meeting under the United States-Chile FTA in November 2012, and two meetings of the NAFTA Committee on Standards Related Measures in February and October.

Regulatory Cooperation Fora

Executive Order 13609

On May 1, 2012, President Barack Obama signed Executive Order (E.O.) 13609 entitled "Promoting International Regulatory Cooperation" to help reduce, eliminate, and prevent unnecessary differences in regulatory requirements imposed by U.S. and foreign regulators, which can limit the ability of American businesses to export and compete internationally. The E.O. calls for the Regulatory Working Group established by E.O. 12866, and reaffirmed by E.O. 13563, to serve as a forum to discuss, coordinate, and develop a common understanding among agencies of

U.S. Government positions and priorities with respect to: international regulatory cooperation activities that are reasonably anticipated to lead to significant regulatory actions; efforts across the Federal Government to support significant, cross-cutting international regulatory cooperation activities; and promotion of good regulatory practices internationally, as well as the promotion of U.S. regulatory approaches, as appropriate.

USTR continues to lead on the coordination and development of standards-related trade policies. The United States participates in three bilateral regulatory cooperation forums aimed at promoting regulatory best practices and aligning regulatory approaches in economically significant sectors with the European Union, Canada, and Mexico.

European Union

The EU's approach to standards-related measures (as described in the 2012 TBT Report), and its efforts to encourage governments around the world to adopt its approach, presents a strategic challenge for the United States in the area of standards-related measures. In 2013, U.S. officials will continue to encourage systemic changes in the EU approach in existing bilateral fora, such as the Transatlantic Economic Council (TEC) and the United States – European Union High-Level Regulatory Cooperation Forum (HLRCF). The TEC is designed to give high-level political direction to bilateral initiatives aimed at promoting increased bilateral trade, job creation, and economic growth through deeper transatlantic economic integration. The HLRCF, comprising U.S. and EU regulatory and policy officials and oversees a program of bilateral cooperation on regulatory issues. The group has convened in advance of each of the previous four TEC meetings to identify projects for the TEC to consider.

In November 2011, the Leaders of the United States and the EU launched the U.S.-EU High Level Working Group on Jobs and Growth (HLWG) with the objective of identifying new ways to increase transatlantic trade and investment in support of job creation, economic growth, and international competitiveness. Leaders directed the HLWG to examine options in specific areas (including possible trade agreements) *inter alia* to reduce and prevent non-tariff barriers.

On February 13, 2013, President Obama and EU leaders announced that they would initiate the internal procedures necessary to launch negotiations on a Transatlantic Trade and Investment Partnership (TTIP). President Obama and EU leaders' announcement followed issuance of the HLWG's final report to leaders (http://www.ustr.gov/about-us/press-office/reports-and-publications/2013/final-report-us-eu-hlwg) in which it recommended that the United States and the EU pursue a comprehensive agreement that would include ambitious, reciprocal market opening in goods, services and investment, make substantial progress on reducing non-tariff barriers, and address global trade issues of common concern. The report's specific recommendations for negotiations on "regulatory issues and non-tariff barriers" include that a comprehensive agreement pursue: SPS and TBT issues; regulatory coherence and transparency; sector-specific outcomes and regulatory cooperation; and the development of a framework for future U.S.-EU progress on the regulatory issues.

Mexico

In May 2010, President Obama and Mexican President Calderón committed to enhance significantly the economic competitiveness and the economic well-being of the United States and Mexico through improved regulatory cooperation. The Presidents directed the creation of a

United States – Mexico High-Level Regulatory Cooperation Council (HLRCC), comprising senior-level regulatory, trade, and foreign affairs officials from each country.

In February 2012, the HLRCC released its first work plan, which outlines cooperative activities on food safety, electronic import and export certificates, oil and gas development, nanotechnology, motor vehicle safety, and e-health and conformity assessment.[45] On October 15, 2012, the HLRCC met to review progress on the seven work plans. It is expected a new consultation schedule will commence in 2013 to update the activities of the HLRCC.

Canada

In February 2011, President Obama and Canadian Prime Minister Harper directed the creation of a United States – Canada Regulatory Cooperation Council (RCC), composed of senior regulatory, trade, and foreign affairs officials from each government. The RCC has a two-year mandate to promote economic growth, job creation, and benefits to U.S. and Canadian consumers and businesses by enhancing regulatory transparency and coordination, with a focus on sectors characterized by high levels of integration, significant growth potential, and rapidly evolving technologies. The United States – Canada Regulatory Cooperation Council (RCC) website provides information on specifics for the 29 initiatives and work plans, including cooperation on topics such as, agriculture, personal care products, pharmaceuticals, and motor vehicles.

The RCC issued a Progress Report to Leaders on December 14, 2012. The report highlighted that work is also underway on the development of Memoranda of Understanding, discussion papers, initial statements of work on regulatory changes, and various assessment activities.

North American Leaders Summit – Trilateral Regulatory Cooperation

The outcomes of the 2012 North American Leaders Summit ("NALS") provide for opportunities for Mexico, Canada, and the United States to promote trilateral regulatory cooperation. Benefits of trilateral regulatory cooperation will include increased economic growth in the three countries; lower costs for their citizens, businesses, producers, governments, and consumers; increased trade in goods and services across borders; and greater protection of health, safety, and the environment.

In 2013, the four sectors that Mexico, Canada, and the United States have agreed upon for trilateral regulatory cooperation are: (1) Regulatory Approach to Nanomaterials; (2) Transportation Railroad Safety; (3) Transportation Emissions; and (4) Globally Harmonized Standards for workplace chemicals.

Doha Round Negotiations

The U.S. Government's longstanding objective in the WTO Non-Agricultural Market Access (NAMA) negotiations – which cover manufactured goods, mining, fuels, and fish products – has been to obtain a balanced market access package that provides new export opportunities for U.S. businesses through liberalization of global tariffs and non-tariff barriers. The NAMA

---

[45] The U.S.-Mexico HLRCC work plan can be found at
http://www.whitehouse.gov/sites/default/files/omb/oira/irc/united-states-mexico-high-level-regulatory-cooperation-council-work-plan.pdf.

negotiations have included discussions of several proposals addressing standards-related measures, including U.S. proposals covering textiles labeling, electronic products, and automobiles.

However, despite continued, intensive efforts by USTR negotiators to engage with key trading partners since the launch of the negotiations, the NAMA negotiations reached an impasse in 2011. In 2012, a new Chairman for the NAMA Negotiating Group was chosen. However, there were no substantive meetings or other activities related to either the tariff or non-tariff elements of the NAMA negotiations, and negotiations on the standards-related non-tariff barrier proposals did not advance.

In 2013, the United States intends to work with other WTO Members to pursue fresh and credible approaches to meaningful multilateral trade liberalization.

X. 2012-2013 Trends Regarding Standards-Related Measures

This section reviews trends that appear across various U.S. trading partners' markets, as well as standards-related systemic issues, that can significantly affect, both positively and negatively, the ability of U.S. businesses and producers to access foreign markets.

Nutritional Labeling and Advertising

In 2011, Thailand became the first country to introduce mandatory front of package (FOP) stop light labeling on food products for five snack categories. In a stop light labeling system, certain nutritional content values are depicted using colors analogous to traffic lights – i.e., red for high, amber for moderate, and green for low. After receiving comments from several WTO members concerning stop light labeling, Thailand opted to implement the Guideline Daily Amount (GDA) system, a guidance system which provides information on to how many calories and nutrients people can consume each day for a healthy, balanced diet. Voluntary schemes are also taking hold in other countries, with South Korea being the first to press ahead with a voluntary scheme for stop light labels on children's foods in January 2011, and reports from the United Kingdom industry indicate that supermarkets will introduce a voluntary, FOP labeling scheme in 2013.

In 2012, several countries in the Western Hemisphere proposed measures related to nutritional labeling and advertising. The most restrictive to date has been Chile's proposed implementing regulations for Law No. 20,606. The Chilean Congress adopted this law on July 6, 2012.

The stated objective of Chile's draft regulation is to provide the public with information about food products in order to prevent obesity and non-communicable diseases. It sets limits for fat (trans fat, saturated fat), calories, sugar, and salt, that if exceeded trigger a requirement to place a stop sign shaped FOP label on the product indicating that the product is "high in" fat, sugar, calories, or salt. The draft regulation requires that the label cover up to 20 percent of the FOP. The draft regulation also imposes certain limits on television advertising of particular foods and restricts the inclusion of promotional toys and related materials in or attached to products.

The mandatory nature of Chile's draft regulation, along with its FOP stop sign labeling requirements, makes it the most far-reaching nutritional labeling requirement of its kind to date. Both Ecuador and Peru are considering similar mandatory and related "high in" claims for prepackaged foods and prepackaged food advertising.

The United States will continue to monitor developments regarding each of these measures and engage in follow-up actions, as appropriate.

EU Agreements on Conformity Assessment and Acceptance (ACAA)

The EU is currently pursuing Agreements on Conformity Assessment and Acceptance of Industrial Products (ACAAs) with several governments in the Mediterranean region, in particular with Algeria, Egypt, Israel, Jordan, Lebanon, Morocco, Palestinian Authority, and Tunisia, as well as Ukraine. Jordan and Israel have already adopted ACAAs with the EU as part of their Euro-Mediterranean Association Agreements with the EU.

The EU ACAAs cover machinery, electrical products, construction products, pressure equipment, toys, medical appliances, gas appliances, and pharmaceuticals. Under these agreements, parties agree to adopt EU standards and regulations in exchange for eased conformity assessment procedures into the EU for certain product sectors.

U.S. manufacturers have expressed concern that the EU ACAAs will create additional export barriers in these regions.

"Voluntary" Measures as Trade Barriers

In various product sectors, certain governments are developing and implementing so-called "voluntary" standards in a manner that effectively makes compliance with them mandatory. In addition, many truly voluntary standards that governments have developed (such as voluntary labeling programs related to energy efficiency or agricultural products) have nonetheless created substantial trade barriers. Further, oftentimes voluntary standards may solely reflect domestic stakeholder interests rather than also those of the larger global trading community.

Examples of "voluntary" standards that have raised trade concerns include:

- China's standards related to information security: The Chinese Government is finalizing several draft "voluntary" standards related to information security for ICT products. The United States is concerned China will make compliance with these voluntary standards mandatory, either through incorporation into technical regulations, or through integration into the certification and type approval schemes of the Ministry of Industry and Information Technology (MIIT) and the CNCA. One such standard, Information Security Technology – Requirement for Office Devices Security, appears to restrict the use of computer chips in ink cartridges. U.S. and other foreign companies consider that this design restriction reduces the functionality of printers, and they question how the measure relates to the protection of national security. U.S. industry and the U.S. Government are concerned that China may effectively mandate the use of this standard by incorporating it by reference into one of China's various certification regimes, for example, the CCC Mark or the MIIT telecom type approval process. U.S. industry is also concerned that various versions of the draft standard, including prohibitions of certain chips as components of printer cartridges, have diverged from the relevant international standard (IEEE 2600).

- Korea's standards for solar panels: Korea's Energy Management Corporation (KEMCO) only certifies one type of thin film solar panel – the type that Korean producers manufacture – as meeting its version of the International Electrotechnical Commission standard. While compliance with that standard is not technically required for sale of solar panels in the Korean market, a company will not be commercially viable in Korea without KEMCO certification. As a result, U.S. solar panel producers that make different kinds of thin film panels find themselves unable to access the Korean market.

As with the other issues identified in this section of the report, the United States works to resolve issues concerning voluntary standards through the TBT Committee and regional and bilateral engagement as they arise in individual markets. The United States is also seeking to address these issues on a systemic basis because many of the specific trade concerns that WTO Members raise in the TBT Committee continue to be related to standards. Currently, U.S. officials are seeking opportunities to tackle the trade issues associated with voluntary standards in the APEC Subcommittee on Standards and Conformance and the TPP negotiations.

Mandatory Labeling of Foods Derived from Genetic Engineering

In May 2011, following twenty years of discussions and negotiations, the Codex Alimentarius Commission (Codex) adopted a "Compilation of Codex Texts Relevant to Labeling of Foods Derived from Modern Biotechnology." The compilation summarizes existing Codex texts and confirms that many Codex labeling guidance documents developed for foods generally also apply to foods derived from modern biotechnology. Most importantly, the compilation confirms that foods derived from modern biotechnology are not necessarily different from other foods simply as a result of the way they are produced. Consistent with that view, the U.S. FDA applies a science-based approach to food labeling, which requires labeling of foods derived from modern biotechnology only if such labeling is necessary to reveal any material information that differs significantly from conventionally produced food in order to avoid misbranding. Such information includes proper use of the food, nutritional properties, and allergens.

The United States continues to be concerned about the European Court of Justice (ECJ) ruling that honey containing pollen with genetically engineered (GE) material should be considered an "ingredient" rather than a natural constituent. As a result, honey with pollen from GE plants would have to be approved under the EU's laws for "genetically modified organisms" and labeled for GE content when sold in the EU. The United States has raised this matter in bilateral meetings with the European Commission. During the March 2012 WTO Sanitary and Phytosanitary Committee meeting, Argentina and Uruguay objected to the ECJ's ruling as creating uncertainty in the markets, which has led to declines in their exports. The United States, Mexico, Brazil, Canada, and Paraguay supported the objections. The Codex standard, upon which the EU based Directive 2001/110/EC, does not treat pollen as an ingredient and the EU was urged to act to withdrawal the measure. In September 2012, the EU Commission proposed an amendment to Directive 2001/100/EC to clarify that pollen is not an ingredient of honey, but it has not been finalized. In addition, the European Food Safety Authority issued an opinion that pollen from the genetically engineered corn approved for cultivation in the EU was equivalent to pollen from conventionally bred varieties of corn. The United States most recently raised this issue during the TBT Committee meeting of March 2013.

The United States is also concerned by a measure proposed by Peru with regards to labeling of foods derived from genetic engineering. Peru renewed its efforts to finalize a regulation mandating that all GE ingredients must be included on the labels of processed products. Peru notified its Draft Supreme Decree Approving the Regulations Governing the Labeling of Genetically Modified Foods to the WTO on June 27, 2011. The regulation requires mandatory labeling of all GE foods even though such products may not differ from non-GE products in terms of safety or quality. The United States submitted comments to Peru on September 14, 2011, but Peru has not responded, and has raised concerns with this measures in several bilateral meetings in 2012 and 2013. The United States (and other WTO Members) raised this issue during the TBT Committee March 2013 meeting as well as during previous meetings.

XI. Country Reports

Background on Specific Trade Concerns Contained in the Country Reports

This section contains individual country reports detailing TBT barriers encountered by U.S. stakeholders. The measures and practices the country reports identify raise significant trade concerns, and, in some instances, give rise to questions concerning whether a trading partner is complying with its obligations under trade agreements to which the United States is a party.[46]

The decisions on which issues to include resulted from an interagency process that incorporated the expertise of a variety of government agencies.

While the tools used to address TBT barriers vary depending on the particular circumstances, in all instances, USTR's goal remains the same: to work as vigorously and expeditiously as possible to resolve the issue in question. As reflected in the country reports, in many instances

USTR seeks to resolve specific concerns through dialogue with the pertinent trading partner – either bilaterally or through multilateral fora – and working collaboratively to obtain changes that result in improved market access for U.S. exporters.

In response to USTR's outreach in compiling this report, stakeholders raised a number of new standards-related concerns. In several cases, USTR lacked sufficient information about those concerns at the time of publication to include them in this report. For purposes of this report, USTR included measures and practices about which USTR is well informed; USTR continues, however, to gather information about others. Accordingly, the omission of any issue in this report should not be taken to mean that USTR will not pursue it, as appropriate, with the trading partners concerned, in the same manner as those listed below. An analysis of the country sections of the 2013 TBT Report demonstrates that numerous issues were recently resolved or are on a path to resolution. Despite these successes, U.S. exporters still face a variety of specific trade concerns as a result of measures adopted or proposed in numerous countries and the EU, as described in the pages that follow.

Argentina

Bilateral Engagement

The United States raises TBT matters with Argentina during TBT Committee meetings.

Testing of All Graphic Products for Lead (Resolution 453)

As previously reported in the 2012 TBT report, the United States continues to be concerned with Argentina's Resolution 453/2010, which requires all inks, lacquers and varnishes used in producing printed materials, such as package labeling and inserts, to undergo testing for lead

---

[46] Nothing in this report should be construed as a legal determination that a measure included in the report falls within the scope of any particular WTO Agreement (*e.g.*, whether the measure is subject to the TBT as opposed to the SPS Agreement).

content. Prior to adoption of an amendment in March 2012 (see below), Resolution 453/2010 required the testing to be conducted in one of two designated laboratories in Argentina. The United States expressed concern during TBT Committee meetings in November 2011 and March 2012 that this regulation appeared to apply to foreign producers only, and that Argentina's testing capacity was insufficient to perform all the required testing. The United States asserted that the situation, coupled with the inability to test these products in the country of production, would lead to significant delays, cost and burdens for industry.

In March 2012, Argentina notified an amendment to Resolution 453/2010. Under this amendment, Argentina will temporarily accept a sworn declaration from the producer or importer that states that the product, or group of similar products, complies with the applicable norm, ASTM D 3335-85a in lieu of testing at the designated laboratories in Argentina. This alternative procedure, however, will be phased out in stages, ending November 12, 2013.

Both the U.S. and the European Union raised this issue during the March and June 2012 TBT Committee meetings. The United States indicated that it continue to question whether mandatory third party certification should be required for these products since they are low risk, and whether it is necessary for the testing to be performed in Argentina itself or by any accredited laboratory. The United States will continue to press Argentina on this issue in 2013.

Electrical and Electronic Products – Conformity Assessment Procedures

Argentina's new requirements for conformity assessment for electrical and electronic products, modifying Resolution 92/98, came into force January 1, 2013, but have not been notified to the WTO. Resolution 92/98 specifies the process by which foreign manufacturers and importers obtain the S-mark safety certification from local certification bodies. This certification is required to market electrical and electronic products between 50 and 1000 Vac in Argentina.

According to U.S. industry, Resolution 92/98 imposes repetitive testing and associated delays, resulting in costs for U.S. exporters that outweigh the purported safety benefits. In addition, industry reports that the requirements disproportionately impact foreign manufacturers and importers and favor domestic manufacturers. Failure to follow Resolution 92/98 will result in the inability of products to clear customs and enter Argentina's market.

The United States will continue to press Argentina on this issue in 2013.

Brazil

Bilateral Engagement

The United States and Brazil discuss TBT-related matters in various bilateral fora, including the bilateral Commercial Dialogue (led by Brazil's Ministry of Development, Industry, and Commerce and the U.S. Department of Commerce), the Economic Partnership Dialogue (led by Brazil's Ministry of External Relations and the U.S. Department of State), and the U.S. - Brazil Commission on Economic and Trade Relations (led by USTR and Brazil's Ministry of Development, Industry and Foreign Trade). The United States also discusses TBT matters with Brazil during TBT Committee meetings.

Health Products

As discussed in previous *TBT Reports*, the United States continues to be concerned with the timeliness of the registration of medical devices in Brazil. Resolutions 24 and 25, notified to the WTO in May 2009 and also known as Public Consultation 11, establish the requirements for manufacturers to submit a Certificate of Good Manufacturing Practice for registration of health products. According to Resolutions 24 and 25, a health product is defined as a product that fits into one of two categories, either a medical product or a product for *in vitro* use diagnosis. As of May 2010, applicants have had to submit to ANVISA a Good Manufacturing Practices (GMP) certificate with their application for registration of health products in Brazil. ANVISA issues a GMP certificate only after it has inspected the manufacturing premises. The United States is aware that Brazil intends to accelerate GMP inspections. However, according to discussions in the 2012 TBT Committee meetings, the average waiting time from submission of the inspection request until completion of the inspection is twenty months, while U.S. industry reports a wait time of up to 3 years. This is significantly longer than the average time of 3 months for similar inspections by other accredited auditing bodies. This delay hinders medical device exports to Brazil.

The United States and other WTO members raised this issue with Brazil in 2012 at meetings of the TBT Committee. The United States pressed ANVISA to accept existing GMP certificates without inspection or to consider subcontracting overseas inspections to accredited auditing bodies. In 2013 the United States will continue to raise this issue with Brazil.

Telecommunications – Acceptance of Test Results

As discussed in the 2012 TBT Report, the United States continues to be concerned about Resolution 323 (November 2002) promulgated by Brazil's National Telecommunications Regulatory Agency (ANATEL). Resolution 323, Standard for Certification of Telecommunications Products, only allows testing of products to be performed within Brazil, except in cases where the equipment is too large or too costly to transport. As a result, U.S. suppliers must present virtually all of their information technology and telecommunications equipment for testing at laboratories located in Brazil before that equipment can be placed on the Brazilian market. This requirement causes redundant testing, higher costs and delayed time to market. Brazil did not notify Resolution 323 to the WTO.

The United States has urged Brazil to implement the CITEL (Inter-American Telecommunication Commission) MRA with respect to the United States. Under the CITEL MRA, two or more CITEL participants may agree to provide for the mutual recognition of conformity assessment bodies and mutual acceptance of the results of testing and equipment certification procedures undertaken by those bodies in assessing the conformity of telecommunications equipment to the importing country's technical regulations. The United States and Brazil are both participants in CITEL. If Brazil implemented the CITEL MRA with respect to the United States, it would benefit U.S. suppliers seeking to sell telecommunications equipment into the Brazilian market by enabling them to have their products tested and certified in the United States to Brazil's technical requirements, eliminating the need for U.S. suppliers to have their products tested and certified in Brazil. The United States will continue in 2013 to encourage Brazil to implement the CITEL MRA with respect to the United States.

Chile

Bilateral Engagement

The United States and Chile discuss TBT-related matters in the context of the United States – Chile Free Trade Agreement, during annual Free Trade Commission and TBT Chapter Committee meetings, as well as during the TBT Committee meetings. The last United States – Chile FTA TBT Chapter Committee meeting was held November 14, 2012.

Food Labeling

The Chile's Congress adopted Law No. 20,606 on nutrition and composition of food and food advertising on July 6, 2012, and according to the Law, it will be implemented on July 6, 2013. Chile notified draft implementing regulations and accompanying guidance on advertising for Law No. 20,606 to the WTO in January 2013. These measures were open for comment until March 2013, and April 2013 respectively. The stated objective of Law No. 20,606 and its implementing regulations is to communicate information to the public about alleged obesity and other non-communicable disease risks in certain food. The proposed regulation requires manufacturers to place a stop sign-shaped icon on the front of the package (FOP) that covers up to 20 percent of the product, if it exceeds limits for fat (trans fat, saturated fat), calories, sugar, and salt. The icon will carry a warning from the Ministry of Health indicating the food is "high in" fat, sugar, calories, or salt. Industry has encouraged Chile to consider existing voluntary programs instead. Trade in processed and packaged foods to Chile amounts to $255 million annually.

The Chilean Ministry of Health responded to requests from and met with domestic and foreign industry members prior to Chile's WTO notification of the measures. Chilean officials also met with U.S. representatives during the November 2012 United States – Chile Free Trade Agreement TBT Chapter Committee meeting, and then again bilaterally in March 2013. The United States raised concerns that the draft regulation is unclear and omits information such as an explanation of how the regulation applies to foods served in restaurants and to existing commercial inventory and whether imports can comply through the use of supplemental labels or stickers. The United States also raised concerns that the labeling scheme as proposed would take up a significant portion of the packaging for some products, that the stop sign shape is unnecessary to communicate the fat, sugar and salt content of the product.

The United States submitted written comments to the Government of Chile on February 26, 2013 through its WTO Inquiry Point regarding the proposed measures, citing similar concerns, including that the draft regulation could have a significant trade impact, that the draft regulation sets out a mandatory labeling requirement when voluntary labeling schemes could address Chile's stated objective, and that the timetable for implementation (July 2013) does not leave sufficient time for industry to comply or address trading partner concerns.

The U.S. Government will continue to monitor the situation and seek opportunities to work with the Chilean government both bilaterally and in the TBT Committee to ensure adequate consideration of comments from stakeholders, a constructive discussion of the rationale, details and potential impact of this proposed regulatory approach, and full consideration of less trade restrictive alternate approaches.

China

Bilateral Engagement

In addition to discussing TBT issues in the TBT Committee, the United States and China regularly engage on TBT-related issues through the United States – China Joint Commission on Commerce and Trade (JCCT) and bilaterally on a case-by-case basis as specific market access issues arise. The JCCT, which was established in 1983, is the main forum for addressing bilateral trade matters and promoting commercial opportunities between the United States and China. The JCCT has played a key role in helping to resolve bilateral TBT issues, including those related to medical device recalls and registration, certification of information technology products, and cotton registration requirements.

Food Additives – Formula Disclosure Requirements

In April, 2011, China's General Administration of Quality Supervision, Inspection and Quarantine (AQSIQ) released its "Specification for Import and Export of Food Additives Inspection, Quarantine and Supervision (2011 No. 52)" ("Specification") The Specification, effective July 1, 2011, appears to require U.S. and other foreign food producers to disclose their proprietary food additive formulas by mandating that food product labels list the precise percentage of each food additive. As a result of this requirement, a competitor would have access to information that it can use to replicate proprietary formulas and compromise an innovator's legitimate commercial interests. The requirement to disclose product formulas appears to apply only to imported food additives.

In addition, China developed and implemented the Specification without notifying the TBT or SPS Committees in advance. As a result, neither the United States nor U.S. industry stakeholders were aware of, or provided the opportunity to comment on, the proposed Specification before AQSIQ issued it. Finally, the measure appears to have taken effect less than six weeks after AQSIQ announced it, which did not provide suppliers with adequate time to comply.

In a May 31, 2012 letter to China, the United States raised concerns regarding the serious impact on legitimate commercial interests caused by the required disclosure of formulas on labels and the apparent application of the Specification only to imported products. The United States observed that the Specification requirements appeared to diverge from the applicable standards in the Codex Alimentarius Commission. The United States also noted that the Specification appeared to conflict with China's own National Food Safety Standard for the Labeling of Prepackaged Foods, which China notified to the WTO in April 2010. China's labeling measure requires only the listing of all ingredients in descending order of in-going weight, and provides that ingredients used in small amounts for the purpose of flavoring need not be declared on the label. The United States emphasized that the regulatory incoherence raised by the Specification created uncertainty in the trading community.

The United States continues to urge China to revise its rules governing food additive disclosures to better align with international standards and to harmonize its food labeling requirements.

China Compulsory Certification (CCC) Requirements – Conformity Assessment Procedures

As previously reported, China's CNCA requires a single safety mark – the CCC mark – to be used for both Chinese and foreign products. U.S. companies continue to report, however, that China is applying the CCC mark requirements inconsistently and that many Chinese-produced goods continue to be sold without the mark. In addition, U.S. companies in some sectors continue to express concerns about duplication of safety certification requirements, particularly for radio and telecommunications equipment, medical equipment, and automobiles.

To date, China has authorized 153 Chinese facilities to perform safety tests and accredited 14 Chinese firms to certify products as qualifying for the CCC mark, as reported in the 2012 USTR Report to Congress on China. When it joined the WTO, China committed to provide non-discriminatory treatment to majority foreign-owned conformity assessment bodies seeking to operate in China. Despite this commitment, China so far has accredited only six foreign-invested conformity assessment bodies. It is not clear whether these six bodies play any appreciable role in testing or certifying products sold in China. China rejected suggestions that it recognize laboratories that have been accredited by ILAC MRA signatories or develop other procedures to recognize foreign conformity assessment bodies. It insists that it will accept conformity assessment bodies domiciled abroad only if the governments of ILAC MRA signatories negotiate MRAs with China. Moreover, China has not developed any alternative, less trade-restrictive approaches to third-party certification, such as recognition of a supplier's self-certification.

Because China requires testing for a wide range of products, and all such testing for the CCC mark must be conducted in China, U.S. exporters are often required to submit their products to Chinese laboratories for tests that may be unwarranted or have already been performed abroad. This results in greater expense and a longer time to market. One U.S.-based conformity assessment body entered into a Memorandum of Understanding (MOU) with China allowing it to conduct follow-up inspections (but not primary inspections) of U.S. manufacturing facilities that make products for export to China requiring the CCC mark. However, China has refused to grant similar rights to other U.S.-based conformity assessment bodies, on grounds that it is prepared to conclude only one MOU per country. Reportedly, both Japan and Germany have concluded MOUs with China that allow two conformity assessment bodies in each country to conduct follow-up inspections.

In 2012, as in prior years, the United States raised its concerns about the CCC mark system and China's limitations on foreign-invested conformity assessment bodies with China both bilaterally and during TBT Committee meetings. At the December 2012 JCCT meeting, China confirmed that eligible foreign-invested testing and certification entities registered in China can participate in CCC mark-related work and that China's review of applications from foreign-invested entities will use the same criteria as those applicable to Chinese domestic entities. The United States will continue to press China on this issue in 2013.

Mobile Devices – WAPI Encryption Standards

The United States continues to have serious concerns regarding China's 2009 unpublished requirement that its WAPI wireless local area networks (WLAN) standard be used in mobile handsets, despite the growing commercial success of computer products in China that comply with the internationally recognized WiFi standard developed by the Institute of Electrical and

Electronics Engineers (IEEE).

In 2011, China's Ministry of Industry and Information Technology (MIIT) remained unwilling to approve any Internet-enabled mobile handsets or similar hand-held wireless devices unless the devices were WAPI-enabled. The United States continued to raise concerns with this requirement, both bilaterally and in TBT Committee meetings.

A new trade concern related to WiFi standards arose in 2011 when China published a proposed voluntary wireless LAN industry standard known as the "UHT/EUHT standard" to be used in wireless networks. China's UHT/EUHT standard appears to be an alternative to the internationally recognized IEEE 802.11n standard. MIIT released the UHT/EUHT standard for a 15-day public comment period on September 20, 2011 and approved it in February 2012. U.S. industry groups commented that the UHT/EUHT standard may not be compatible with either WAPI or the IEEE 802.11 standard. Separately, the United States expressed its concern to China that the integration of the UHT/EUHT standard into certification or accreditation schemes would make the standard effectively mandatory. This could restrict market access for U.S. producers. The United States will vigorously pursue a resolution of this issue in 2013.

Mobile Devices – Draft Regulatory Framework

China's MIIT issued the "Draft Mobile Smart Terminal Administrative Measure" ("Measure") on April 10, 2012. The Measure established a new regulatory framework for the mobile device market. The United States raised concerns about the Measure with China in April and May 2012. The United States expressed concern that the Measure imposed numerous new obligations, technical mandates, and testing requirements on information technology and telecommunications hardware, operating systems, applications, app stores, and other related services. The scope and mandatory nature of these requirements appear unprecedented among the major global markets for mobile smart devices.

On June 1, 2012, MIIT published a draft of the Measure on its website, soliciting public comment for 30 days. In addition, in November 2012, China notified the draft measure to the TBT Committee and indicated that it would accept comments for a 60-day period. Both the United States and affected industry submitted written comments on the Measure. The United States and U.S. industry are concerned that the top-down government-mandated requirements contained in the Measure are overly burdensome and could create significant trade barriers. Furthermore, the United States and U.S. industry are concerned that inclusion in the Measure of numerous voluntary standards and testing requirements relating to smart terminals could create additional trade barriers if these voluntary standards become mandatory through MIIT's testing and certification process. At the December 2012 JCCT meeting, China confirmed that it will take the views of all stakeholders into full consideration in regard to the regulation of information technology and telecommunications hardware, operating systems, applications, app stores, and other related services. The United States and China will continue to discuss this issue as China revises the current draft.

4G Telecommunications - ZUC Encryption Algorithm Standard

At the end of 2011 and into 2012, China unveiled an encryption algorithm (known as the ZUC standard), which was developed by a quasi-governmental Chinese research institute for use in 4G Long Term Evolution (LTE). The European Telecommunication Standards Institute (ETSI)

3rd Generation Partnership Project (3GPP) had approved ZUC as one of three voluntary encryption standards in September 2011. According to U.S. industry reports, MIIT, in concert with the State Encryption Management Bureau (SEMB), informally announced in early 2012 that only domestically-developed encryption algorithms, such as ZUC, would be allowed for the network equipment (mobile base stations) and mobile devices comprising 4G TD-LTE networks in China. In addition, industry analysis of two draft ZUC-related standards published by MIIT suggests that burdensome and invasive testing procedures threatening companies' sensitive intellectual property could be required.

In response to U.S. industry concerns, the United States urged China not to mandate any particular encryption standard for 4G LTE telecommunications equipment used on commercial networks, in line with its bilateral commitments and the global practice of allowing commercial telecommunications service providers to work with equipment vendors to determine which security standards to incorporate into their networks. The United States stated that any mandate to use a domestic encryption standard such as ZUC would appear to contravene a commitment that China made to its trading partners in 2000, which clarified that China would permit the use of foreign encryption standards in IT and telecommunication hardware and software for commercial use and that it would only impose strict "Chinese-only" encryption requirements on specialized IT products whose "core function" is encryption. Additionally, a ZUC mandate would appear inconsistent with China's 2010 JCCT commitment on technology neutrality. In 2010, China had agreed to take an open and transparent approach that allowed commercial telecommunication operators to choose which telecommunications equipment and encryption technologies and standards to use for their networks and not to provide preferential treatment to domestically-produced standards or technology used in 3G or successor networks, so that operators could choose freely among whatever existing or new technologies might emerge to provide upgraded or advanced services.

The United States pressed China on this issue throughout the run-up to the December 2012 JCCT meeting. At that meeting, China agreed that it will not mandate any particular encryption standard for commercial 4G LTE telecommunications equipment. In 2013, the United States will continue to closely monitor developments in this area.

IT Products – Multi-Level Protection Scheme

Beginning in 2010 and continuing through 2012, both bilaterally and during TBT Committee meetings, the United States has raised concerns with China about its framework regulations for information security in critical infrastructure known as the Multi-Level Protection Scheme (MLPS), issued in June 2007 by the Ministry of Public Security (MPS) and MIIT. The MLPS regulations put in place guidelines to categorize information systems according to the extent of damage a breach in the system could pose to social order, the public interest, and national security. The MLPS regulations also appear to require buyers to comply with certain information security and encryption requirements that are referenced in the MLPS regulations.

MLPS regulations bar foreign products from being incorporated into Chinese information systems graded level 3 and above. (China grades an information system with respect to its handling of national security information, with the most sensitive systems designated as level 5). Systems labeled as grade level 3 and above, for instance, must solely contain products developed by Chinese information security companies and their key components must bear

Chinese intellectual property. Moreover, companies making systems labeled as grade level 3 and above must disclose product source codes, encryption keys, and other confidential business information. To date, government agencies, firms in China's financial sector, Chinese telecommunications companies, Chinese companies operating the domestic power grid, educational institutions, and hospitals in China have issued hundreds of request for proposals (RFPs) incorporating MLPS requirements. These RFPs cover a wide range of information security software and hardware. By incorporating level-3 requirements, many RFPs rule out the purchase of foreign products.

Currently, China applies the MLPS regulations only in the context of these RFPs. If China issues implementing rules for the MLPS regulations to apply the rules broadly to commercial sector networks and IT infrastructure, those rules could adversely affect sales by U.S. information security technology providers in China. The United States urged China to notify the WTO of any MLPS implementing rules promulgating equipment-related requirements. At the December 2012 JCCT meeting, China indicated that it would begin the process of revising the MLPS regulations. It also agreed to discuss concerns raised by the United States during the process of revision. The United States will continue to urge China to refrain from adopting any measures that mandate information security testing and certification for commercial products or that condition the receipt of government preferences on where intellectual property is owned or developed.

Medical Devices – Conformity Assessment Procedures

The United States has expressed concerns over the past years regarding China's medical device registration requirements. China has not notified proposed revisions to Order 276 "Regulation on Supervision and Administration of Medical Devices" to the WTO. Amendments to Order 276 have been under consideration by the Legislative Affairs Office of the State Council and significant revisions were released in 2007, 2010, and in 2012.

The most recent 2012 revision (third draft) of Decree 276 continues to mandate country-of-origin registration, a requirement that prevents foreign manufacturers of medical devices from registering their products in China without prior marketing approval in the country of origin or country of legal manufacture. According to U.S. industry, this requirement has blocked or inordinately delayed sales of safe, high-quality medical devices to the Chinese market because some manufacturers did not apply for marketing approval for certain products in the countries in which they were produced or in their home countries for reasons unconnected with product quality or safety. For example, producers may design particular medical devices specifically for patients in a third country, such as China, or may choose to produce them in a third country for export only. In these situations, a manufacturer would have no business reason to seek to have a particular device approved in its home country or the country of export and would likely forego that process in order to avoid the associated burdens of time and money. China continues to defend this requirement despite concerted efforts to resolve this issue. The United States will continue to press the issue in 2013.

Draft revisions to Order 276 also continue to reflect: 1) problematic product type testing (or "sample testing") requirements; 2) a burdensome re-registration process; and 3) the requirement that clinical trials be repeated in China in order to register products there. Industry continues to advocate for the transition from end-product type testing to a Quality Management System approach, as outlined in ISO standard 13485. Furthermore, while the latest draft increases the validity of a registration from four to five years, China's re-registration process continues to require fees and submissions comparable to the initial registration process.

With respect to the issue of in-country clinical trials, at the 2010 JCCT Subgroup meeting, China's State Food and Drug Administration (SFDA) committed to accept clinical evidence from outside China and that China would not automatically mandate in-country clinical trials for Class II and Class III devices. However, the latest revision of Decree 276 proposed a waiver of in-country clinical trials for Class I (lowest risk) devices only and remains unclear on potential waivers of clinical trials for Class II and Class III devices. In bilateral discussions with China in 2012, the United States urged China to meet with stakeholders to discuss their concerns. The United States will continue to monitor the development of revisions to Order 276 in 2013.

Imaging and Diagnostic Medical Equipment – Classification

Another source of concern relates to China's classification of imaging and diagnostic medical equipment. China classifies most imaging and diagnostic medical equipment as Class III. This classification represents the highest risk and therefore it is the most stringent classification for medical devices. This classification is problematic because it deviates from international practices and burdens manufacturers with additional requirements, such as conducting expensive and potentially unnecessary domestic clinical trials.

During the 2011 JCCT meeting, the United States urged China to place certain imaging and diagnostic medical equipment into a lower risk category. China's SFDA committed to issue, by June 2012, a complete list of x-ray equipment to be placed in a lower risk category and agreed to endeavor to release a draft for an *in vitro* (*e.g.,* test tube) diagnostic equipment catalog for public comment by June 2012. Subsequently, in August 2012, SFDA revised and lowered the classification for four sub-categories of imaging and diagnostic medical equipment under the "Classification Catalogue of Medical Devices," including certain medical ultrasonic instruments and related equipment, medical x-ray equipment, medical x-ray ancillary equipment and components, and medical radiation protective equipment and devices. The United States will work in 2013 to ensure that China fully implements its commitment.

Patents Used in Chinese National Standards

In the State Council's Outline for the National Medium to Long-Term Science and Technology Development Plan (2006-2020) and in the 11th Five Year Plan (2006-2010) for Standardization Development of the Standardization Administration of China (SAC), China prioritized the development of national standards.

In November 2009, SAC circulated for public comment proposed "Provisional Rules Regarding Administration of the Establishment and Revision of National Standards Involving Patents." The provisional rules indicated that in principle a mandatory national standard should not incorporate patented technologies. The draft provisional rules also indicated that when the use of patented technologies was needed a compulsory license could result if the relevant government entity was unable to reach agreement with the patent holder. The United States provided comments opposing this and other aspects of the draft provisional rules, which did not take effect. In December 2012, SAC circulated new draft interim measures, omitting certain troubling aspects of the earlier draft, such as the compulsory license provision, but raising other concerns, including in its definition of the responsibilities and potential liabilities of individuals and organizations that participate in the formulation of revision of national standards. In early 2013, the United States provided comments to SAC on these and other concerns. The United States will continue to engage with China on this issue in 2013.

Electronic Information Products – Certification of Pollution Control

The United States continues to be concerned by China's Administrative Measures for Controlling Pollution Caused by Electronic Information Products, issued by MIIT and several other Chinese agencies effective March 2007. This measure (known as "China RoHS") is modeled after existing European Union regulations. While the regulations of both China and the EU seek to ban lead and other hazardous substances from a wide range of electronic products, there are significant differences between the two regulatory approaches.

China's original RoHS regulations were developed without any formal process for interested parties to provide input to MIIT and were not timely notified to the TBT Committee. As a result, stakeholders outside China had limited opportunity to comment on proposals or to clarify MIIT's implementation intentions. The regulations omitted basic information, such as the specific products subject to mandatory testing and the applicable testing and certification protocols. Industry in the United States and other countries expressed concern that producers would have insufficient time to adapt their products to China's requirements and that in-country testing requirements would be burdensome and costly. China circulated subsequent proposed revisions to its RoHS regulations in 2010 and in 2012. U.S. industry submitted comments on the July 2012 draft revision.

Concurrent with these developments, China issued the catalog of electronic information products subject to hazardous substance restrictions and mandatory testing and conformity assessment under the China RoHS regulations. The final version of the catalog included mobile phones, other phone handsets, and computer printers. Information on the applicable testing, certification, and conformity assessment regime was not included in either the draft or final catalog. MIIT and CNCA also introduced a voluntary program in November 2011 to certify electronic information products to the China RoHS limits established for six substances. The United States will carefully monitor developments in this area in 2013.

Cosmetics –Approval Procedures and Labeling Requirements

SFDA initiated a series of changes to China's cosmetics regulation after obtaining jurisdiction over the industry in 2008. SFDA imposed additional requirements on "new ingredients" in April 2010, and promulgated guidance on the application and evaluation of new cosmetic ingredients in 2011. These actions stalled the approval of cosmetics containing new ingredients. In fact, SFDA has approved only a handful of new ingredients since 2010. The United States, along with EU and Japan, continue to raise concerns regarding the application requirements at TBT Committee meetings.

In December 2012, China notified "Cosmetics Label Instructions Regulations" and "Guidance for the Cosmetics Label Instructions," which propose new labeling requirements that are in addition to the two existing labeling requirements that apply to cosmetic products. In January 2013, industry submitted comments through the U.S. TBT Inquiry Point, arguing that the proposed regulation overlaps and conflicts with existing Chinese regulations, as well as creates an undue burden for the industry.

The United States is also monitoring possible implications of SFDA's efforts to create an inventory of "existing ingredients" that have been approved for use in cosmetics products in China. In September 2012, SFDA released for comment the "SFDA Notification: List of Raw Materials Already in Use in Cosmetics (Third Batch)." The first and second lists of materials were released in April and July 2012, respectively.

The United States will urge China to continue dialogue with all interested parties regarding these measures and to take into account the comments received. China should also consider alternative measures that are more commensurate with the risks involved, such as post-market surveillance and reliance on internationally-recognized good manufacturing practices (GMPs). These alternatives would meet China's legitimate regulatory objectives with fewer disruptive effects on international trade.

Colombia

Bilateral Engagement

The United States discussed TBT matters with Colombia during and on the margins of TBT Committee meetings, and in the TBT Chapter Committee of the United States – Colombia FTA. The first meeting of this committee was held October 23-24, 2012.

Distilled Spirits – Identity Requirements

Prior *TBT Reports* outlined U.S. industry's concerns over the quality and identity requirements that Colombia proposed in 2009 for distilled spirits, including gin, rum, vodka, and whiskey.

On August 24, 2012, Colombia notified to the WTO a final version of its alcoholic beverage regulation, which contained standards of identity for distilled spirits based on analytical parameters, such as a limit on congeners and other naturally occurring constituents of gin, vodka, and rum. The regulation provides for a 12-month transition period. Unlike Colombia's approach, the standards of identity for distilled spirits sold in the United States, the European Union, Canada, and nearly every other major spirits market bases their standards of identity on the raw materials and processes used to produce distilled spirits. In response to Colombia's notification, the United States submitted written comments expressing concern about Colombia's approach of basing identity requirements on chemical composition rather than raw materials and processes used to produce the distilled spirits. The United States will continue to monitor this issue in 2013.

Commercial Vehicles – Diesel Emissions

As raised in prior *TBT Reports*, the United States remains concerned about the Ministry of the Environment and Sustainable Development's draft resolution amending Resolution No. 910 of 2008. On December 14, 2012, the Government of Colombia notified this proposed measure to the WTO. Amended Resolution No. 910, which is proposed to go into effect August 5, 2013, indicates that the current commercial vehicles emission standards in Colombia, EPA 98 (a U.S. standard) and EURO III (an EU standard), will not be valid for new commercial vehicles seeking registration for sale in Colombia and that EPA 04 and EURO IV emission standards will be accepted for long haul semitrailers until December 2014. The draft resolution further provides that by January 2015, all commercial vehicles seeking registration for sale in Colombia must meet EURO IV emission standard requirements. Given the design of some U.S.-manufactured diesel truck engines, industry has expressed concern that use of this EU standard would effectively exclude many U.S. heavy duty trucks from the Colombian market. Further, according to EcoPetrol, the Colombian state-run oil company, the fuel necessary to comply with the standard will not be available nationwide until 2017. This situation is exacerbated by the fact that engines designed to meet EPA 04 standard, which is more stringent than the EURO IV standard, already face restricted access to the Colombian market, because Colombia does not maintain adequate supplies of the high-quality fuel needed for these high technology engines.

The United States has encouraged Colombia to focus efforts on removing older trucks from the road to achieve the most immediate and significant emissions reductions. In 2012, the United States raised concerns during the first meeting of the United States – Colombia FTA TBT Committee meeting, engaged in technical exchanges, and raised the issue on the margins of the March and June TBT Committee meeting.

In 2013, the United States will respond to the WTO notification of the draft resolution, and will continue to raise concerns about the measure bilaterally and in the WTO.

The European Union

Bilateral Engagement

The United States has actively engaged the EU on TBT-related matters in the TBT Committee, the WTO Trade Policy Review of the EU, and in bilateral meetings. The United States also raises concerns and encourages reform in EU approaches to key TBT issues in the Transatlantic Economic Council (TEC) and the United States – European Union High-Level Regulatory Cooperation Forum (HLRCF).

In addition, the United States and the EU work together to promote the importance of maintaining open and transparent regulatory and standards development processes in emerging markets, as well as jointly advocating on specific market access issues on behalf of US and EU exporters.

The announcement by President Obama and EU leaders that the United States and the EU intend to pursue a comprehensive trade and investment agreement will provide new opportunities to address TBT-related issues with the EU.

Honey – Biotechnology Labeling

EC Regulation No. 1829/2003 addresses GE crops for food use and for animal feed. The United States, along with other WTO Members, has expressed concerns in TBT Committee meetings, most recently in March 2013, regarding the requirement in Regulation No. 1829/2003 that honey containing pollen derived from GE plants must be labeled as such in accordance to EU regulations. This requirement was the result of the ECJ 2011 decision in Case C-442/09 that interpreted EC Regulation No. 1829/2003. The United States will continue to monitor this issue in 2013. In September 2012, the EU Commission proposed an amendment to Directive 2001/100/EC to clarify that pollen is not an ingredient of honey, but it has not been finalized. In addition, the European Food Safety Authority issued an opinion that pollen from the genetically engineered corn approved for cultivation in the EU was equivalent to pollen from conventionally bred varieties of corn. The United States raised this issue during the March 2013 TBT Committee meeting.

In addition, industry has raised concerns on several occasions about the impact the EU's restrictive stance on biotechnology has had on U.S. exports of soy, grains, corn, and other crops. The United States have repeatedly raised concerns and objections with the EU regarding the EU's biotechnology regulations and legislation and their detrimental effect on U.S. exports. With respect to SPS issues arising from the EU's policy regarding food and agricultural products derived from modern biotechnology, please refer to the SPS Report.

Accreditation Rules

As noted in previous *TBT Reports*, the United States has serious concerns regarding the EU's accreditation framework set out in EC Regulation No. 765/2008. The regulation, which became effective in January 2010, requires each Member State to appoint a single national accreditation body and prohibits competition among Member States' national accreditation bodies. The regulation further specifies that national accreditation bodies shall operate as public, not-for-profit entities.

Under the regulation, Member States can recognize non-European accreditation bodies at their discretion. Member States may refuse to recognize non-European accreditation bodies and refuse to accept conformity assessments issued by these bodies. The regulation raises market access concerns for U.S. producers, whose products may have been tested or certified by conformity assessment bodies accredited by non-European accreditation bodies.

The United States will continue to press the EU on these issues in 2013.

Foods - Quality Schemes

New framework legislation for quality schemes in agriculture, EU No. 1151/2012, became effective in January 2013. The quality schemes provide for (1) "certification" procedures, in which detailed specifications are checked periodically by a competent body and (2) "labeling" systems to communicate information regarding product quality to the consumer, and which are subject to official controls. The United States is concerned with an element of the legislation that establishes a new framework for the development and protection of optional "quality terms." For example, it creates and protects the term "mountain product."

In particular, the United States is concerned that the legislation incorporates commonly used terms into the EU's quality schemes and subjects them to registration requirements. The United States is concerned that, as result, the legislation will negatively impact U.S. producers' ability to export and market their products in the EU. The United States will seek to work with the EU to address these concerns in 2013.

Chemicals – REACH Regulation

The EU's REACH regulation imposes extensive registration, testing, and data requirements on tens of thousands of chemicals. REACH also subjects certain chemicals to an authorization process that would prohibit them from being placed on the EU market except for specific uses. U.S. industry is concerned that REACH requires polymer manufacturers and importers to register reacted monomers in many circumstances. This is problematic because reacted monomers no longer exist as individual substances in polymers and would not create exposure concerns in the EU. In addition, EU polymer manufacturers generally can rely on the registrations of their monomer suppliers and do not need to be individually registered. Since U.S. monomer suppliers are generally not located in the EU, U.S. polymer producers cannot likewise rely on registrations of their monomer suppliers. As a result, the reacted monomer registration requirement provides an incentive for distributors to stop importing polymers and switch to EU polymer suppliers. The United States has pressed the EU to eliminate the registration requirement.

Moreover, REACH contains notification and communication obligations with respect to substances on the Candidate List, a list of substances that may become subject to authorization procedures. Differing interpretations between the Commission and several Member States regarding when these obligations apply has created uncertainty among industry over how to comply. The Commission has indicated that notification and communication obligations apply if a substance on the Candidate List is present in an article in concentrations above 0.1 percent of the article's entire weight. However, Member States have stated that these obligations should apply when a substance on the Candidate List is present in concentrations above 0.1 percent of the weight of the article's components or homogenous parts. In 2010, these Member States pushed the Commission to reverse its position as part of what may have been an effort to seek to protect the EU market from imports. Departure from the Commission's interpretation would present a much more difficult compliance problem for U.S. industry since it would require companies to perform an analysis of individual component concentration levels in their products, which would be extremely time-consuming and burdensome. Given that an alteration of the EU's approach could substantially disrupt U.S. exports, the United States has asked the EU to ensure that all Member States follow the Commission's current interpretation.

Other problematic issues with the EU's REACH regime include inadequate transparency and differing registration requirements for EU and non-EU entities. In general, the European Commission regularly publishes notices of draft EU measures in the Official Journal of the European Union and sends notifications to the WTO Secretariat. However, U.S. and other non-EU interested persons allege such notifications occur far too late in the process for them to familiarize themselves with the new requirements and submit timely comments. In advance of these notifications, European Commission trade and regulatory officials consult primarily with EU stakeholders.

The United States has raised concerns regarding REACH at nearly every TBT Committee meeting since 2003, and has been joined by many other WTO Members, including Argentina, Australia, Brazil, Canada, Chile, China, Colombia, Cuba, the Dominican Republic, Ecuador, Egypt, El Salvador, India, Israel, Japan, Korea, Malaysia, Mexico, Qatar, Russia, Singapore, Switzerland, Taiwan, and Thailand. The United States also has raised its concerns regarding REACH directly with the EU and has worked with the European Chemicals Agency on specific technical issues.

In addition, the United States registered concerns with the EU during the November 2011 TBT Committee meeting regarding a costly REACH requirement, applied only to manufacturers outside the EU, to appoint "Only Representatives" (ORs). An OR is a natural or legal person established in the EU authorized to carry out the obligations that REACH imposes on importers. REACH bars U.S. producers from registering substances for use in the EU and thus they must engage an OR for this purpose.

The United States also encouraged the EU to address in its 2012 REACH review data compensation issues in connection with the operation of Substance Information Exchange Forums (SIEFs). Specifically, U.S. industry has raised concerns that the "lead registrant" for each SIEF may take commercial advantage of its position in dealing with other SIEF members, particularly SMEs. Because other SIEF members must negotiate with the lead registrant to register their chemicals, a lead registrant could unfairly charge members registration fees at a level that would reduce competition in the EU market. The United States urged the EU to consider issuing guidance for cost-sharing that would place limits on what lead registrants can charge other SIEF members, thus preventing undue financial burdens on those members, especially SMEs.

The United States will continue to monitor closely REACH implementation in 2013, and will raise trade concerns, as appropriate, in the TBT Committee and other pertinent fora.

Wine – Traditional Terms

The EU continues to seek exclusive use of so-called "traditional terms" such as tawny, ruby, reserve, classic, and chateau on wine labels, but may allow third-country producers to use such terms if their governments enter into an agreement with the EU regulating use of the terms in their markets. Regulation EC No 607/2009 implements EU protections on designations of origin and geographical indication, traditional terms, labeling, and presentation of certain wine products.

The EU's regulation of traditional terms severely restricts the ability of non-EU wine producers to use common or descriptive and commercially valuable terms to describe their products sold in the EU. While no shipments have been blocked, U.S. industry reports that the regulation has deterred exporters from seeking to enter the EU market. The EU's efforts to expand the list of so-called "traditional terms" to include additional commercially valuable terms are also problematic because some of these terms do not have a common definition across all EU Member States. Additionally, the United States remains concerned about the EU's decision to withdraw permission to use certain "traditional terms" under the United States – EU agreement on trade in wine, as well as the EU's limitation on the use of traditional expressions in trademarks.

The EU justifies these above-mentioned efforts to limit use of traditional terms on the ground that misuse of the terms may confuse consumers. However, these terms have been used without incident on U.S. wines in the EU market for many years. Moreover, the EU has allowed the use of the terms by other countries, including Chile, South Africa, Canada, and Australia. Although the EU recently approved the use by U.S. industry of the terms "cream" and "classic" it has not issued a decision with respect to use on U.S. products of the terms "chateau," "clos," "ruby," and "tawny." During 2013, the United States will continue to coordinate with U.S. wine exporters on how best to address and resolve concerns regarding the EU's wine policy, and will engage with EU officials at the TBT Committee and in bilateral meetings.

Distilled Spirits – Aging Requirements

The EU requires that for a product to be labeled "whiskey" it must be aged a minimum of three years. U.S. whiskey products that are aged for a shorter period cannot be marketed as "whiskey" in the EU market or other markets such as Israel and Russia that adopt EU standards. The United States views a mandatory three-year aging requirement for whiskey as unwarranted. In fact, recent advances in barrel technology enable U.S. micro-distillers to reduce the aging time for whiskey. Variations in climate can also shorten aging time. In 2013, the U.S. will continue to urge the EU and other trading partners to end whiskey aging requirements that serve as barriers to U.S. exports.

Biofuels – Renewable Energy Directive

The EU's renewable energy directive (RED) provides for biofuels (such as biodiesel and ethanol) and biofuel feedstocks (such those derived from soybeans or canola) to be counted toward fulfilling Member State biofuel use mandates. It also provides for biofuels and biofuels feedstocks to benefit from RED tax incentives but only if they qualify for a sustainability certificate. However, to qualify for a sustainability certificate biofuel or biofuel feedstock must meet a patchwork of standards or be subject to a bilateral agreement with the EU. The use of varying approaches and sustainability standards has disrupted U.S. trade in soybeans.

To find alternative approaches to address U.S. concerns with the EU's certification scheme, the United States and the EU began discussions to explore a possible bilateral agreement that would recognize that longstanding U.S. conservation programs correspond to RED sustainability criteria. In July 2011, a high-level delegation from the U.S. Government met with officials from the EC Directorate-Generals for Trade and Energy to address U.S. concerns. Additional discussions were held in September, November, and December 2011, leading to the creation of a working group to explore the possibility of a bilateral agreement as provided for under the RED. The working group met in February, April and June 2012, but did not reach agreement on the basis for a bilateral agreement. In the November 2012 TBT Committee meeting, the United States continued to urge the EU to show flexibility and openness in recognizing different approaches that could provide equivalent outcomes when it comes to sustainable energy feedstocks. In 2013, the United States will continue to work with the EU and push for resolution of U.S. concerns.

India

Bilateral Engagement

The United States discusses TBT matters with India in various fora including the TBT Committee, the United States – India Trade Policy Forum (TPF), the United States – India Commercial Dialogue, and the High-Technology Cooperation Group. The United States and India also engage in ad hoc bilateral discussions. For example, the United States and India conducted a digital video conference on standards and conformity assessment on December 12, 2012. Similar conferences are planned for 2013.

In addition, the Confederation of Indian Industry (CII) and ANSI have added India-specific content on relevant standards, conformity assessment, and technical regulations in India to ANSI's standards portal.

Cosmetics – Registration Requirements

In April of 2008, India notified to the WTO an amendment to its "Drugs and Cosmetics (Amendment) Rules of 2007" that introduced a new registration system for cosmetics products that U.S. industry believes to be overly burdensome and costly, and lead to unnecessary delays to market for companies' products.

In 2009 and 2010, U.S. industry sought clarifications in a number of areas, and India made a number of modifications to the measure and developed implementing guidelines. The United States raised the issue at the June 2012 TBT Committee meeting. In particular, the United States expressed concern that under the guidelines the registration certificates and import licenses for foreign producers must be renewed every three years, while the certificates and licenses for domestic producers are valid for five years.

India has not yet addressed these concerns and has indicated that the guidelines will enter into force on March 31, 2013. In 2013, the United States will continue to monitor the implementation and changes to the guidelines and press for changes that address U.S. concerns.

Foods Derived from Biotech Crops

India's biotechnology regulatory and approval system prohibits the importation of food and agricultural products containing ingredients derived from biotech crops such as corn and soybeans, with soybean oil being the sole exception.

On June 5, 2012, India's Department of Consumer Affairs proposed an amendment to the Legal Metrology (Packaged Commodities) Rules, 2011 that would require, *inter alia*, that the term "GM" be placed on the principal display panel of packages containing genetically engineered foods.

The United States will continue to monitor this issue in 2013.

Telecommunications Equipment – Information Security Regulations

In 2009 and 2010, India imposed new requirements in telecommunications service licenses, including mandatory transfer of technology and source codes as well as burdensome testing and certification for telecommunications equipment. Following extensive engagement with trading partners including the United States, India eliminated most of these requirements in 2011. In doing so, however, India adopted new telecommunications license amendments that continue to require, among other things, that as of April 2013, testing of all telecommunications equipment deemed to raise security concerns take place in India. The U.S. Government and industry continue to press India to reconsider the domestic testing policy and to adopt the international best practice of using international common criteria and accepting products tested in any accredited lab, whether located in India or elsewhere.

The United States will continue to monitor this issue in 2013.

Toys and Toy Products – Registration and Testing Requirements

The United States continues to be concerned about the proposed "Toys and Toy Products (Compulsory Registration) Order" being considered by the government of India. As noted in the *2012 TBT Report*, the registration order, if implemented, would impose onerous and time consuming registration obligations on U.S. toy companies and conformity assessment burdens that are dramatically higher than those found in any other country.

The proposed manufacturer's self-declaration provisions require an extremely detailed and onerous level of information, including submission of a registration form that contains information concerning management composition, raw materials, components, machinery (including the serial numbers for all equipment on the factory floor and notification whenever a piece of equipment is removed from the factory, even for maintenance), factory layout, production processes, packing/storage, inspection, and quality control staff for each plant at which the imported toys are manufactured. Much of this information is unnecessary as it does not demonstrate anything about the quality or safety of the toy nor the quality of the manufacturing process.

In addition, the proposed rule requires test reports on samples of any toy or toy product conducted by a Bureau of Indian Standards (BIS)-recognized laboratory in India or by an overseas laboratory that has a mutual recognition agreement with BIS, of which there are none. Test reports from ILAC-accredited laboratories are not accepted under this proposed rule. As noted in the *2012 TBT Report*, it appears India's safety objectives are currently – and can continue to be – achieved by accepting test results from internationally recognized laboratories, such as ILAC-accredited laboratories.

Indonesia

Bilateral Engagement

The United States discusses TBT matters with Indonesia both bilaterally and during TBT Committee meetings. The United States – Indonesia TIFA Council provides a forum for bilateral discussions on a variety of trade-related issues, including standards-related issues. The United States and Indonesia also participate actively on standards and conformance issues through APEC.

Horticulture Products – Labeling Requirements

In September 2012, Indonesia issued Ministry of Agriculture's (MOA) Regulation 60 and Ministry of Trade's (MOT) Regulation 60 (amending MOT Regulation 30). These regulations impose a broad range of requirements on the importation of horticultural products into Indonesia and include provisions related to labeling. MOA's Regulation 60 requires that MOA consider the "packaging requirement and labeling in Indonesian," among other considerations prior to issuing a "recommendation for the import of horticultural products" or RIPH. MOT's Regulation 60 contains labeling and packaging requirements. For instance, the regulation requires that Bahasa Indonesia labels be attached to the packaging prior to entering the Indonesian customs area. Indonesia did not notify these regulations to the TBT Committee.

The United States raised concerns about the labeling and packaging requirements contained in these measures at the November 2012 TBT Committee, as well as in numerous bilateral meetings. The United States requested that a WTO dispute settlement panel be established regarding MOT regulation 60 and MOA regulation 60, as well as other regulations in connection with their import licensing and quantitative restrictions in March 2013. The United States will continue to raise concerns in 2013 regarding the labeling aspects of the measures.

Processed Foods – Bahasa Labeling Requirement

In September 2010, Indonesia's National Agency for Drug and Food Control (BPOM) announced that it would require all imported processed food products to be labeled exclusively in the Bahasa language and require the labels to be affixed to product containers prior to "entering Indonesian territory" effective March 1, 2011. Indonesia agreed to a U.S. request to delay enforcement until March 1, 2012. Also in response to U.S. concerns, Indonesia agreed to accept supplemental Bahasa language labels in lieu of original, exclusive Bahasa language labeling.

In June and July 2012, Indonesia notified two new BPOM regulations to the TBT Committee, G/TBT/N/IDN/60 and G/TBT/N/IDN/59, laying out new requirements for registration and labeling for processed foods. Together, the measures establish an extensive and complex registration system for processed food products and burdensome labeling requirements, including mandating the disclosure of confidential and proprietary information and requiring unnecessary warning statements for products containing colorants and artificial sweeteners. At the November 2012 TBT Committee, the United States raised concerns and asked that Indonesia delay enforcement until after comments from interested parties could be taken into account. The U.S. submitted written comments in August 2012.

Effective January 2013, Bahasa language labeling before entering Indonesia is required. However, enforcement is done via signed statements from importers stating that labeling requirements are met. BPOM conducts periodic checks at importers' warehouses since they are not allowed to enter customs areas. In 2013, the United States will continue to raise concerns regarding these requirements.

Food, Supplements, Drugs, and Cosmetics – Distribution License Requirements

In 2009, BPOM announced licensing requirements for companies that distribute food, health food supplements, drugs, and cosmetics in Indonesia, including imported products. Although the proposed licensing requirements vary by product type, they all could significantly disrupt trade. For example, imported food distributors would be required to provide reference letters from the overseas production facility, certifications for health or *halal* status, and a certificate stating that the production process was radiation free. The United States raised concerns about the proposed licensing requirements with Indonesia bilaterally and in TBT Committee meetings. BPOM issued a proposed replacement regulation in early 2011, which addresses some of the potentially burdensome requirements. For example, the revised proposal no longer requires *halal* certificates for products that do not claim to be *halal* consistent. The United States will continue to raise concerns with this regulation with Indonesia.

Toys – Standards and Testing Requirements

In 2012, Indonesia's Directorate General of Manufacturing Industries proposed to enforce a recently enacted toy safety standard, SNI 8124:2010. The U.S. toy industry is concerned that the safety standard will require redundant and burdensome in-country testing. The United States raised concerns regarding SNI 8124:2010 bilaterally and in TBT Committee meeting in 2012. At the request of the United States, Indonesia notified the draft decree to the WTO in July 2012, as G/TBT/N/IDN/64. The United States is encouraging Indonesia, in lieu of in-country testing, to allow foreign suppliers to provide laboratory test reports by ILAC- accredited laboratories. Recognition of test results from ILAC-accredited laboratories is common international practice in the toy sector, prevents market-access delays, and reduces the burden on local testing and certification facilities. The United States also raised concerns over the requirement that toys be affixed with a mark indicating compliance with SNI ISO 9001:2008. Indonesia has responded that it is in the process of developing technical guidance concerning the requirement. The United States will remain engaged on this subject as Indonesia develops its guidance and continue to press Indonesia to accept testing performed by ILAC-accredited laboratories.

Japan

Bilateral Engagement

The United States discusses TBT issues with Japan bilaterally, including through the United States – Japan Economic Harmonization Initiative (EHI) established in November 2010, as well as in multilateral fora such as the TBT Committee.

Organic Product Requirements

During 2012, the United States actively engaged Japan through a series of bilateral meetings to address outstanding issues regarding trade in organic products, and initiate negotiations towards increasing bilateral trade in these products. These meetings have facilitated the technical exchange needed to bring U.S. concerns closer to resolution, and the United States and Japan are engaged in the negotiation of a possible mutual organic equivalence arrangement.

While the negotiations are underway, the United States continues to raise specific concerns with Japan. In contrast to U.S. organic standards, Japan will not certify as organic any agricultural products produced with alkali extracted humic acid or lignin sulfonate. Humic acids are used in farming to improve soil structure, increase water retention, promote seed germination, and improve yields. Lignin sulfonate is used as a flotation device for cleaning fresh fruits.

The United States also continues to express concern that Japan does not allow the use of the Japan Agriculture Standard (JAS) organic logo in conjunction with U.S. logos. In addition, Japan does not allow USDA certified products to affix the JAS logo in the United States, unless the certifier is JAS accredited. The product must instead be imported into Japan by a JAS accredited importer who then affixes the required JAS organic logo. The cost of doing this in Japan adds additional cost to the product. This topic is being discussed in the equivalency negotiations.

The United States will continue to work closely with Japan to address these concerns through the negotiation process and hopes to improve access to Japan's market for U.S. organic products.

Kenya

Bilateral Engagement

The United States discusses TBT matters with Kenya both bilaterally and during TBT Committee meetings. The United States – East African Community (EAC) TIFA Council also provides a forum for bilateral discussions of standards-related issues.

Alcoholic Beverages – Labeling Requirement

As noted in the *2012 TBT Report*, Kenya previously notified in 2011 labeling requirements, the "Alcoholic Drinks Control (Licensing) Regulations," for alcoholic beverages. The requirements, which are presently suspended because of domestic litigation, could prove onerous to U.S. exporters if they go into effect. For example, one of the requirements is that a warning message comprise at least 30 percent of the package's surface area.

In December 2012, Kenya notified to the WTO proposed revisions to the measure. The revisions appear to make some positive changes, such as removing the restriction that foreign broadcasts and publications cannot promote alcoholic beverages, however, the revision still requires that a warning message appear on the package although there is uncertainty as to its required size. In January 2013, the United States requested clarification on the size of the warning label and stated that the requirement to change the warning statement every 100 bottles appears to be overly restrictive and burdensome.

The United States will continue to closely monitor this issue in 2013.

Korea

Bilateral Engagement

Korea and the United States regularly discuss TBT issues through bilateral consultations. The consultations serve as an important forum for discussing and resolving these issues and are augmented by a broad range of senior-level policy discussions. In June 2012, the United States and Korea held bilateral trade consultations leading to the resolution of a number of TBT issues, such as avoiding duplicative electrical safety testing and the adoption of the latest international standard for electronic devices and providing a one-year grace period for new cosmetic labeling regulations to allow industry time to adjust. In addition, the United States raises TBT issues with Korea during and on the margins of TBT Committee meetings. Opportunities for bilateral engagement on TBT issues will continue to increase through the work of the TBT Committee and an Automotive Working Group, established under the United States – Korea Free Trade Agreement, which entered into force on March 15, 2012.

Cosmetics – Labeling

In August 2012, the National Assembly proposed legislation that would require labeling for all packaging of all cosmetics products despite existing exemptions for small packages under 10 ml or grams. U.S. companies will potentially encounter a considerable financial burden if the bill is enacted into law. Consequently, the United States will continue to monitor this issue in 2013.

Chemicals – Act on the Registration and Evaluation of Chemicals (REACH)

In February 2011, Korea's Ministry of Environment (MOE) released a draft "Act on the Registration and Evaluation of Chemicals (REACH)" to the National Assembly. As announced, Korea REACH would create a complex registration system for chemical products, perhaps as early as 2014. U.S. industry submitted comments to MOE on Korea's proposal, and the United States raised this issue with Korea bilaterally and in the TBT Committee in June and November 2011.

In 2012, Embassy Seoul monitored the draft Act and continued to discuss concerns about the burden and lack of clarity of Korea's proposed Act, in particular the draft law's proposed *de minimis* level of 0.5 tons (rather than the EU REACH one ton) and duplicative reporting requirements. Many of these concerns, including the *de minimis* level and reporting requirements, were addressed in the version of the Act that MOE submitted to the National Assembly in September 2012. The Act has not been approved by the National Assembly, and the legislature continues to work with the MOE to refine the legislation; it is unclear whether areas in which MOE reflected industry comments will all be maintained in the final law. The United States seeks to ensure that Korea's final requirements are not unnecessarily trade-restrictive.

In 2013, the United States will continue to monitor developments related to the proposed registration system and urge Korea to take U.S. industry's comments into account.

Organic Products – Requirements and Conformity Assessment Issues

Korea's Act on Promotion of Eco-Friendly Agriculture and Management of Organic Products (the "Organic Products Act") becomes effective on May 29, 2013. The Organic Products Act clarifies requirements previously adopted in 2008 for organic certification and labeling that mandate certification of processed organic products by a certifier accredited by the Ministry of Food, Agriculture, Fisheries, and Forestry (MIFAFF). Under the new requirements, U.S. organic products would need to be re-certified to maintain their organic labeling. Many U.S. producers and certifiers are reluctant to seek product re-certification due to the difficulty of ensuring that individual ingredients also meet certification requirements. However, the Organic Products Act permits the conclusion of equivalence agreements, which might alleviate burdens on U.S. products. Nevertheless, the Organic Products Act does not permit equivalence agreements to go into effect until January 2014. The United States, Canada, Australia, New Zealand, and the European Union requested Korea to suspend its new certification and labeling requirements until equivalence agreements can be concluded. On November 13, 2012, Korea agreed to this request and will permit foreign organic products to be labeled as organic in Korea without MIFAFF-accredited certification. The United States seek to initiate discussions negotiations with Korea on an equivalency agreement in 2013 with the view to concluding an arrangement that will facilitate exports of U.S. organic products.

Information Technology Equipment – Electrical Safety Regulations

U.S. industry has been working closely with KATS and the Radio Research Agency on the reorganization of safety regulations for information technology equipment. The United States has advocated for streamlined procedures that reflect the realities of contemporary manufacturing and would provide an appropriate level of safety certification for low-risk information technology equipment, such as printers and computers. KATS amended its regulations in July 2012, addressing many of the U.S. concerns, such as expanding the scope of products subject to a supplier's declaration of conformity, and adopting the most current IEC standard. However, some concerns remain unaddressed. For example, the regulation does not allow for safety certifications to be made by a single multinational enterprise for all identical products; rather, the regulation requires separate certification with respect to each factory's products. Currently, there is also no certificate renewal process. Furthermore, despite being a member of the IECEE CB scheme, KATS is not currently accepting CB reports without additional testing.

We will continue to raise this issue with Korea in 2013.

Solar Panels – Testing Requirements

Korea requires solar panels to be certified by the Korea Management Energy Corporation (KEMCO) before they can be sold in Korea in projects receiving government support (which means in practice the vast majority of sales). KEMCO's certification standards prevent certain types of thin-film solar panels manufactured by U.S. industry from entering the Korean marketplace. For example, KEMCO has established a standard for thin film solar panels that can only be satisfied by panels manufactured from amorphous silicon. As a result, other leading types of thin film solar panels made by U.S. firms, including Cadmium Telluride (CdTe) and Copper Indium (di) Selenide (CIS), cannot be tested or certified under the Korean standard and thus remain shut out of most of Korea's market. The United States urged Korea at the 2012 bilateral trade consultations and at TBT Committee meetings to adopt the relevant international standard, IEC 61646, without limiting its application solely to the type of thin-film solar panel its industry produces. If Korea did so, it would both facilitate trade and afford Korean consumers access to the best available technologies.

In response to U.S. concerns, Korea conducted an environmental impact review on the use of cadmium in solar panels, and determined that a hazard existed for using CdTe, while the hazard of CIS was relatively small. Korea has said it will consider developing a new certification standard for CIS based on the results of that study. U.S. industry has raised methodological concerns with the studies Korea used to disqualify CdTe. The United States will continue to raise this issue with Korea in 2013.

Motor Vehicle Parts - Safety Standards and Certification

In August 2011, Korea published draft regulations for comment, which mandated that specified replacement motor vehicle parts comply with Korea Motor Vehicle Safety Standards (KMVSS) and established a self-certification system for indicating compliance with the safety standards. The final regulation, promulgated in December 2011, reflected some of the comments submitted by the foreign automotive industry but did not reflect important requests related to the acceptance of parts certified to non-Korean standards. In April 2012, Korea published draft administrative guidelines, which contained implementation details for the new system and which raised additional concerns related to the allowable methods for marking the parts. The United States worked closely with Korea over several months on these proposed measures and U.S. concerns regarding use of non-KMVSS standards for parts and allowable methods for marking parts were resolved.

In 2013, we will continue to monitor the implementation of these measures.

Cellular Phones – Specific Absorption Rate (SAR) Labeling

In October 2012, Korea published and notified draft technical regulations that would establish two labeling categories for SAR levels (absorption of electromagnetic radiation) for mobile phones. Korea allows phones with a SAR level of 1.6 W/kg or less to be marketed in Korea. The proposed regulation, however, would establish two tiers within the allowable range: phones with a SAR of 0.8 W/kg or less would be labeled as "Level 1," while phones with a SAR between 0.8 and 1.6 W/kg would be labeled "Level 2." U.S. industry has submitted comments on the regulation raising concerns that there is no clear rationale or scientific basis for distinguishing between phones that meet the relevant safety regulation, and that the label could mislead, rather than inform, consumers by suggesting that there is a safety difference between the two categories. The United States has raised this concern with Korea in bilateral consultations and we will continue to do so 2013.

Malaysia

Bilateral Engagement

The United States discusses TBT matters with Malaysia during TBT Committee meetings, bilaterally on the margins of those meetings, and during TPP negotiations. The United States and Malaysia also participate actively on standards and conformity assessment issues through APEC.

Meat and Poultry Products – Halal Standards

Malaysia requires all domestic and imported meat (except pork) to be certified as *halal* (produced in accordance with Islamic practices) by Malaysian authorities. Malaysian regulations require producers' *halal* practices to be inspected and approved for compliance with Malaysian standards on a plant-by-plant basis prior to export.

In January 2011, Malaysia implemented a food product standard – MS1500: 2009 – that sets out general guidelines on *halal* food production, preparation, handling, and storage. MS1500: 2009 creates standards that go well beyond the internationally recognized *halal* standards, which are contained in the Codex Alimentarius. Specifically, the guidelines require slaughter plants to maintain dedicated *halal* production facilities and ensure segregated storage and transportation facilities for *halal* and non-*halal* products. In contrast, the Codex allows for *halal* food to be prepared, processed, transported, or stored using facilities that have been previously used for non-*halal* foods, provided that Islamic cleaning procedures have been observed.

In April 2011, Malaysia notified to the WTO its "Draft Malaysian Protocol for the Halal Meat and Poultry Productions." The protocol provides additional information and guidance on complying with MS 1500: 2009. In May 2011, the United States provided comments on the protocol and subsequently raised concerns regarding the protocol during the June and November 2011 TBT Committee meetings. Following that, Malaysia scheduled mandatory audits for establishments seeking to export to Malaysia. These audits took place in September 2012. The

United States recently received notice from Malaysian officials that only one U.S. establishment passed the audit. All the other establishments failed the audits and are accordingly prohibited from exporting to Malaysia.

Additionally, in early 2012, Malaysia changed its pet food requirements such that porcine ingredients are now banned from food for cats, which many Malaysians keep as pets. Malaysia did not notify this change to the WTO, nor has Malaysia produced satisfactory justification for this prohibition, other than to indicate it will help consumers avoid purchasing products with porcine (i.e. non-*halal*) ingredients. Malaysia has not begun to enforce these requirements yet. The United States has suggested that Malaysia's objectives could also be achieved through alternative measures such as labeling.

The United States will continue to pursue all *halal* related concerns with Malaysia in 2013.

Mexico

Bilateral Engagement

The United States discusses TBT matters with Mexico during TBT Committee meetings and on the margins of these meetings. The United States and Mexico also engage on standards and regulatory issues in the NAFTA Committee on Standards-Related Measures, which met in February and October of 2012, and as part of the United States – Mexico High-Level Regulatory Cooperation Council, which was established in 2010, and issued a Work Plan in February 2012.

Energy Efficiency Labeling

In September 2010, Mexico's Secretariat of Energy published the "Catalogue of equipment and appliances used by manufacturers, importers, distributors and marketers that require mandatory inclusion of energy consumption information." The Catalogue was notified to the TBT Committee in June 2011 and imposes labeling obligations for manufacturers, importers, distributors, and marketers of those products. The labels to be placed on the products must contain information regarding the product's energy efficiency and confirming that the product meets certain testing requirements. U.S. industry has raised concerns that the scope of the products subject to the catalog's labeling requirements remains unclear. Accordingly, U.S. industry has requested that Mexico delay implementing the catalog until those issues are resolved. The United States raised these concerns with Mexico both bilaterally and in the June and November 2011 TBT Committee meetings. Furthermore, in 2012, the U.S. and Mexican governments met on numerous occasions to discuss how to better align the two countries' energy consumption labeling regulations and energy efficiency policies.

Although the catalog entered into force in September 2011, it has not been enforced. Mexico did engage with U.S industry to clarify the catalog's requirements. However, the United States will seek to identify product categories that can be removed from the catalog due to their *de minimis* energy consumption. The United States will continue to engage Mexico on this issue in 2013.

Sanitation Pipes – Standards

As noted in prior *TBT Reports*, the United States is concerned that Mexico's National Water

Commission (NWC) has not recertified U.S. producers of certain plastic pipe for waste water systems, drinking water systems, and domestic service connections, under the Mexican standard applicable at the time (NOM-001-CONAGUA-1995).[47] According to industry, NWC has instead sought to enforce an obsolete ISO standard on high density polyethylene (HDPE) plastic pipe, that is not incorporated into the Mexican standard and that relies on design and descriptive characteristics, rather than performance abilities. Furthermore, although both HDPE pipe and polyvinyl chloride (PVC) pipe – a competing product – cannot satisfy the design characteristics of the this ISO standard, NWC appears to only be enforcing this standard on HDPE pipe and not PVC pipe, the latter of which is manufactured predominantly by the domestic industry. Industry reports that HDPE pipe meets the standard contained in NOM-001-CONAGUA-199, as well as relevant performance characteristics as described in other, more up-to-date, state-of-the-art international standards.

The United States has raised this issue with Mexico both bilaterally and in the TBT Committee, and continues to request that Mexico ensure that the standards NWC adopts are applied on a non-discriminatory basis, are science-based, and are developed through transparent processes as required by the TBT Agreement. Additionally, the United States has encouraged Mexico to apply the Mexican standard as written. On February 17, 2012, CONAGUA released an amended mandatory standard, NOM-001-CONAGUA-2011, which authorizes acceptance and use of standards that are utilized in the markets of Mexico's trading partners, including the United States. Under this standard, U.S. pipe manufacturers, therefore, appear entitled to recertification under standards utilized in the United States, including ASTM International standards F2764, F2736, and F2947. However, despite accepting U.S. HDPE manufacturers' requests for recertification and the completion of relevant testing, in February 2013, NWC stated that it still cannot recertify HDPE plastic pipe because NWC has been unable to confirm that ASTM International is an internationally recognized standard setting body, notwithstanding that the amended mandatory standard does not appear to limit the standards for recertification to only those produced by internationally recognized standards setting bodies and that ASTM International is generally recognized as an internationally recognized standard setting body.

Medical Device – Equivalency

In October 2010, Mexico published an executive order related to article 194B of the General Health Law that would streamline conformity assessment procedures for shipments of medical devices and certain over-the-counter (OTC) drugs from the United States. Under these rules, any producer or importer of medical devices or equipment can obtain a sanitary registration within 35 days, provided that U.S. regulators have approved the product for sale. The Mexican regulator, Federal Commission for Protection Against Sanitary Risks ("COFEPRIS") has had difficulties in implementing this process and has been working with industry to improve implementation. While some progress has been observed, numerous U.S. companies continue to complain about excessive wait times of one to two years for sanitary registration approval.

---

[47] Mexico has since amended NOM-001 several times. The most recent amendment, NOM-001-CONAGUA-2011, was notified to the WTO in February 2012.

In October 2012, COFEPRIS announced the implementation of an agreement that will expedite the registration in Mexico of new pharmaceutical products already reviewed and approved by regulatory agencies in the United States, Australia, Canada, Switzerland and the EU. According to COFEPRIS, the agreement will promote public health in Mexico by giving Mexican consumers access to innovative pharmaceutical products approved for sale in the United States and elsewhere. In addition, COFEPRIS asserts that agreement will reduce from 360 days to 60 days the approval time for certain drugs.

The United States will continue to monitor the implementation of the Agreement in 2013.

Vitamin Supplements – GMP Certification

In August 2008, Mexico issued an administrative decree amending articles 168 and 170 of the Regulation for Health Supplies, which required Good Manufacturing Practices (GMP) certification by Mexican certifiers for foreign companies that sought to sell pharmaceutical and nutritional supplements in Mexico. GMPs are production and testing practices meant to ensure the quality level of a product. In January 2010, U.S. officials requested that Mexico clarify its compliance requirements for vitamin supplements and other products marketed as nutritional supplements in the United States. Because the FDA does not issue export certificates to confirm compliance with GMPs for supplements, the United States has asked whether COFEPRIS would accept either a manufacturer's self-declaration of GMP compliance or a GMP certificate issued by a third-party certifier. COFEPRIS has indicated it allows third party certification by COFEPRIS authorized certifiers or local/state authorities.[48] The United States will continue to ask COFEPRIS to consider third-party certification by non-COFEPRIS authorized certifiers or perhaps conducting manufacturing facility inspections in the United States.

Russian Federation

The Russian Federation is a Party to the Russia-Kazakhstan-Belarus Customs Union (CU) as well as the Eurasian Economic Community (EurAsEC). Technical regulations, standards, and conformity assessments systems in Russia are governed by the CU's Eurasian Economic Commission, as well as at the national level. The CU Parties as well as the Members of EurAsEC have agreed to harmonize their policies and regulatory systems in the TBT arena.

On August 22, 2012, Russia became the 156th Member of the WTO. Russia's entry into the WTO brought the largest market outside of the WTO into the global trading regime's rules-based organization. Russia pledged to liberalize its trade regime to create an open and level playing field, thereby increasing its transparency and predictability.

In 2012, the United States commented on the Ministry of Economic Development's Decree on determining the criteria for notifying technical regulations and establishment of its WTO TBT Inquiry Point. In 2013, the United States will continue to emphasize the importance of timely notifications of draft technical regulations to the WTO, to ensure the availability of reasonable comment periods on draft regulations and reasonable implementation periods for final regulations, as well as a clear point of contact for each notification.

---

[48] State health departments in the United States do not issue GMP certificates for supplements.

Russia made its first two WTO TBT notifications on December 21, 2012. The first notification, by the Ministry of Industry and Trade, was "Amendments to the Technical Regulation of the Customs Union on Safety of Wheeled Vehicles," and the second was the "EurAsEC Technical Regulation on Alcohol Product Safety". The latter was notified only after a specific request by WTO Members, and did not provide a comment period. The United States will continue to urge Russia to be forthcoming in making its notifications to the WTO Secretariat for both technical regulations and amendments.

Bilateral Engagement

The United States will work with Russia in the TBT Committee and bilaterally through the Business Development and Economic Relations Working Group (BDERWG) established under the United States – Russia Bilateral Presidential Commission. The BDERWG provides a forum for the United States and Russia to discuss, *inter alia*, standards-related regulatory cooperation. In 2013, the United States and Russia will look to increased engagement, as a matter of priority, in the area of standards and conformity, launching programs to understand better each other's standards and regulatory structures, find areas for increased cooperation, and eliminate unnecessary obstacles to trade.

Food – Labeling Requirements

In October 2012 the Eurasian Economic Commission (EEC) of the CU published a revision to the "Technical Regulations on Food Products Labeling." The revision imposes numerous labeling requirements, including with respect to nutritional components, allergens, and GE foods. In addition, the revision requires that products containing sweeteners must carry a warning statement that overuse will cause digestive problems, and those products with food coloring must declare that it affects children's ability to concentrate. This revision was not notified to the WTO. While implementation of these rules is scheduled for July 1, 2013, the EEC will allow products labeled under the previous regulations to circulate in the market until February 15, 2015. The United States sent comments to the EEC in December 2012. The comments expressed concern that the revised regulations require labeling for GE products and nutritional components beyond the recommended guidelines established in the Codex General Standard for Food Labeling. Additionally, the United States noted that the requirements for labeling of allergens in food are unclear. These claims are not based on the latest scientific research nor do they appear consistent with the Codex. The United States has not received a response to its December 2012 comments. In 2013, the United States will continue to engage the EEC in 2013 to resolve outstanding concerns.

Alcoholic Beverages – "Strip Stamps"

As noted in last year's *TBT Report*, Russia levies excise taxes on alcohol and enforces these taxes through a system that requires alcohol beverage containers to bear an excise "strip stamp" label. Over the last year U.S. industry has reported some positive improvements with respect to Russia's strip stamp requirements, including advanced notice and comment of requirements and a more effective transition from the use of old stamps to new stamps with an adequate grace period and functioning electronic registration.

Alcoholic Beverages – Conformity Assessment Procedures, Standards, and Labeling

The EEC revised its "Technical Regulation on Alcoholic Product Safety" in November 2012, and included some positive changes, including removing a requirement mandating the aging of rums and reducing the size of the warning statement to allow for other consumer and branding information on containers.

However, the United States still has significant concerns with the EEC draft "Technical Regulation on Alcoholic Product Safety" which is proposed to enter into force in July 2013. Most notably, the proposed measure would impose duplicative conformity assessment procedures, administered by at least three different government authorities, all of which appear to have the same objective of data registration. Specifically the proposed requirements call for a new alcohol beverage notification procedure to be administered in Russia by the Federal Service for the Regulation of the Alcohol Market. U.S. industry is concerned that the multiple conformity assessment procedures administered by different agencies add an unnecessary level of complexity leading to increased costs and time delay. Furthermore, the United States is aware that Russia, outside of the work of the EEC, has passed a law (Amendment SF171) which contains another similar notification procedure for alcoholic beverages. It is scheduled to go into effect on March 1, 2013. The United States has requested that Russia postpone implementation of SF171.

The EEC "Technical Regulation on Alcoholic Product Safety", also introduces burdensome and unique requirements to label all alcoholic beverages, with an expiration date, or include a label indicating that "the expiry date is unlimited if the storage conditions are observed." U.S. industry notes that the proposed requirement does not provide accurate or beneficial information for products containing more than 10 percent alcohol, because these products do not expire. Furthermore, the proposed expiration date requirement appears inconsistent with international guidelines – particularly with Article 4.71(vi) of the Codex General Standard for the Labeling of Prepackaged Foods, which exempts beverages containing 10 percent or more by volume of alcohol from such date-marking requirements. The United States will encourage Russia to eliminate this requirement for alcoholic beverages containing more than 10 percent alcohol by volume, and urge Russia to adopt international standards or guidelines.

The proposed technical regulation gives rise to other issues that could affect U.S. exports of alcoholic beverages, including unclear definitions for wine and wine beverages and a requirement that whiskey be aged no less than three years. In February 2013, the United States provided comments the EEC and will continue to work with Russia on this matter.

Alcoholic Beverages - Warehousing Requirements

The United States has been engaged with Russia on its storage requirements for alcoholic beverages. Those storage requirements are set forth in Regulation Order #59n. As a result of bilateral discussions that took place in 2011, Russia issued a revised regulation in 2012, which offered some improvements, such as the removal of the requirement that pallets be 15 mm high from the floor. However, outstanding issues remain. For example, the United States seeks clarification regarding the specificity of warehouse construction requirements, the stringency of warehouse inspections, and temperature controls, which appear to exceed international standards. The United States provided comments to Russia in August 2012. As of February 2013, the United States has yet to receive a response. The United States also raised concerns in the WTO about the revised requirements with Russia during the November 2012 TBT Committee, and urged Russia to provide timely and transparent inspections, because distilled spirits manufacturers continue to experience costly delays awaiting inspection approvals.

South Africa

Bilateral Engagement

The United States and South Africa discuss TBT matters during TBT Committee meetings, bilaterally on the margins of these meetings, and under the United States – South Africa Trade and Investment Framework Agreement. USDA and the South African Department of Agriculture, Forestry and Fisheries (DAFF) discuss TBT matters through their annual bilateral forum in Pretoria, South Africa.

Liqueurs – Alcohol Content Restrictions

In 2009, U.S. industry expressed concerns about South Africa's classification of alcoholic beverages. Alcoholic products cannot be sold in South Africa unless they fall within a designated classification, which is determined in part by alcohol content. South Africa classifies "liqueurs" as beverages having a minimum alcohol content of 24 percent and classifies "spirit coolers" as beverages having 15 percent or less alcohol by volume (ABV). South Africa does not maintain any classification for spirit-based alcoholic beverages with an alcohol content of between 15-24 percent, with the exception of products that fall into the "Cream Liqueur" classification, namely spirit-based alcoholic beverages that contain a dairy product, or "Cocktail/Aperitif" classification, beverages based on herbs or other flavorings of vegetable origin that differ from wine with alcohol volume content between 15 and 23 percent by volume. As a result, any U.S. products that fall in the gap between the "liqueur" and "spirit cooler" classifications, and outside the Cream Liqueur or Cocktail/Aperitif classification, cannot be sold in South Africa.

Not only have these requirements kept certain U.S. products out of the market, but industry has reported that South Africa may not be applying its requirements equally to domestic and imported products. In particular, U.S. importers have reported that South Africa granted at least one exception to a domestic product containing 15-23 percent alcohol level by volume.

During 2013, the United States will continue to raise concerns regarding South Africa's alcoholic beverage standards and, if appropriate, will urge South Africa to eliminate or modify its "liqueur" definition, or seek another solution that facilitates trade, such as an exemption, so that U.S. alcoholic beverage producers can sell their products in South Africa.

Taiwan

Bilateral Engagement

The United States discusses TBT matters with Taiwan during TBT Committee meetings and bilaterally on the margins of these meetings as well as under the auspices of the United States – Taiwan Trade and Investment Framework Agreement (TIFA).

Ceiling Panels – Requirements for Incombustibility Testing Methods

As discussed in the *2012 TBT Report*, U.S. companies that manufacture finished interior building materials, such as ceiling panels and wood paneling, continue to raise concerns regarding the testing method that Taiwan mandates for determining whether those materials meet applicable incombustibility requirements. According to U.S. industry, Taiwan's present measure gives U.S. ceiling tiles a lower incombustibility rating than is otherwise warranted. In some instances, U.S. ceiling tiles unreasonably fail the test altogether. The reason the testing is problematic according to U.S. industry is that Taiwan's measure applies a variation of the ISO 5660 standard for Reaction to Fire Tests - Heat Release, Smoke Production and Mass Loss Rate, which at the time was not complete; however, U.S. industry notes that a recent revision of the ISO standard incorporated additional guidelines that will ensure better and more reliable incombustibility ratings and should therefore be adopted by the Taiwan authorities as soon as possible. In October 2012, USTR urged Taiwan to adopt the ISO committee's revised standard. USTR continues to monitor Taiwan's process in adopting a standard mirroring the revised ISO 5660 (released in January 2013 as ISO 5660-3).

Commodity Goods – Labeling Requirements

As discussed in the 2012 report, the United States raised concerns that Taiwan requires all "commodity goods" (consumer goods) to be labeled with the manufacturer's or producer's name, telephone number, and address. In addition to concerns over protecting proprietary information under the requirements of such labeling, industry notes that some commodity goods are produced by several different manufacturers and product labels may not be large enough to contain all of the required information. This measure imposes costs for firms, including the cost of developing unique labeling requirements for the Taiwan market.

U.S. officials have raised these concerns with Taiwan's representatives, including on the margins of the TBT Committee meetings as well in staff-level meetings under the TIFA. We will continue to monitor this issue in 2013.

Product Multipacks – Labeling Requirements

U.S. industry has raised concerns over a reinterpretation by Taiwan's Ministry of Economic Affairs (MOEA) of its "Commodity Inspection Act" and "Commodity Labeling Act" in 2006 to require all units included in a retail multipack to be labeled for individual sale, even if the retailer will not divide up the multipack for sale as single units. U.S. suppliers have asserted that this requirement imposes unnecessary additional costs as it forces them to add additional labels on their products to continue exporting to Taiwan.

U.S. officials raised this issue with their Taiwan counterparts during TBT Committee meetings and most recently in an October 2012 TIFA working-level meeting. Taiwanese officials responded that Taiwanese consumers typically purchase bulk items such as socks in individual units rather than multipacks and therefore that individual units included in multipacks must be labeled to avoid the risk of fraudulent country of origin labeling. U.S. officials requested that Taiwan notify the WTO of its revised labeling rules to provide an opportunity for WTO Members to submit comment. MOEA has yet to do so.

Turkey

Bilateral Engagement

The United States discusses TBT matters with Turkey during, and on the margins of, TBT Committee meetings, in meetings of the Council established under the United States – Turkey Trade and Investment Framework Agreement (TIFA), in United States – Turkey Economic Partnership Commission (EPC) talks, and in the bilateral cabinet-level Framework for Strategic Economic and Commercial Cooperation (FSECC). The FSECC is designed to reinforce the work of the EPC and TIFA and provide political-level guidance on particularly challenging commercial and economic issues.

Pharmaceuticals – GMP Decree

In late 2009, Turkey's Ministry of Health issued a "Regulation to Amend the Regulation on the Pricing of Medicinal Products for Human Use," which took effect on March 1, 2010. The regulation requires foreign pharmaceutical producers to secure a Good Manufacturing Practice (GMP) certificate based on a manufacturing plant inspection by Turkish Ministry of Health (MOH) officials, before their products can be authorized for sale in Turkey.

The United States, although it does not oppose MOH inspection requirements for pharmaceutical manufacturing facilities, has concerns with respect to this measure. Specifically, the United States is concerned that Turkey did not publish or notify this regulation to the WTO. In addition, the United States is concerned that Turkey no longer accepts U.S. FDA's GMP certifications, and that pharmaceutical producers face significant delays in meeting the inspection requirements because of the MOH's extensive backlog of GMP inspections. In the February 2013 bilateral Trade and Investment Framework Agreement meeting, Turkey stated that it would consider amending its regulatory practices in order to allow MOH's review of the pharmaceutical product dossier to take place concurrently with the pharmaceutical producer's process of obtaining GMP certification.

While we still need to monitor progress in 2013, this is potentially a significantly positive step, which the United States encouraged using various engagement opportunities in 2012.

Food and Feed Products – Mandatory Biotechnology Labeling

In 2009, Turkey's Ministry of Agriculture published a regulation governing biotechnology in food and feed. The measure was not publicly announced or notified to the WTO in advance of entry into force, and contained no phase-in period. Turkey has since published several amendments to the regulation and later superseded this regulation with the enactment of the "Biosafety Law," which was notified to the WTO. This Law became effective in September 2010 and mandates the labeling of ingredients derived from biotechnology in all food and feed if the biotechnology content exceeds a certain threshold, a requirement that impedes U.S. food and feed exports to Turkey. In addition, Turkey's Biosafety Law goes beyond mandatory method-of-production labeling, which refers to the mandatory labeling that a product or ingredient in a product was produced using biotechnology. The labeling requires that "GMO" labels on food should contain health warnings if the biotechnology food differs from the non-biotechnology food.

This labeling requirement raises additional concerns because it appears to presume, incorrectly, that food containing biotechnology products is inherently more risky from a health perspective than its non-biotechnology food counterpart. Consequently, such health warnings could unnecessarily cause public alarm while providing no additional public health protection. For example, changes in edible oil composition could lead to health benefits, and the oil could still be as safe for consumption as similar oils. Thus, the use of health warnings in the absence of a legitimate health concern could misinform the public about food safety.

In addition to the labeling requirement, the Biosafety Law mandates strict traceability for all movement of biotechnology feed and includes onerous requirements for each handler to maintain traceability records for 20 years. The United States has engaged bilaterally with Turkey in the margins of the TBT Committee meetings on issues related to Turkey's Biosafety Law. The United States will continue bilateral talks on these issues with Turkey in 2013.

Vietnam

Bilateral Engagement

The United States discusses standards-related issue with Vietnam during TBT Committee meetings and on the margins of TPP negotiations, as well as through the bilateral United States – Vietnam TIFA Council meetings. The United States also works with Vietnam in advancing standards and conformity assessment issues through ASEAN and APEC.

Food Safety Law – Registration Requirements for Processed Foods

The United States has concerns regarding Decree 38, the implementing regulation for Vietnam's Food Safety Law, which was signed into law in June 2012. The measure was notified to the SPS Committee in March 2011, and was notified to the TBT Committee in December 2012. Under the measure, exporting manufacturers of prepackaged processed foods, food additives and food packaging materials must complete numerous forms and certificates to obtain affirmations of the product's conformity to Vietnamese laws and regulations. Products without these conformity assessments may not be exported to Vietnam.

Although the implementation date for Decree 38 was June 11, 2012, implementation has been gradual as the various ministries involved sort out their responsibilities and enforcement activities. The United States, along with other WTO Members, has requested that enforcement of the Decree, as well as any subsequent implementing regulations, be delayed until the specific concerns of the United States and other trading partners can be fully addressed.

At the June 2012 TBT meeting, the United States raised concerns about Decree 38 with support from Australia, the EU, New Zealand, Canada, and Chile, and also submitted extensive written comments and technical questions to Vietnam at that time. The United States continued to raise concerns with Vietnam over Decree 38 throughout 2012, both at the November 2012 TBT meeting and in Hanoi.

The United States will continue to monitor the issue and raise concerns with Vietnam in 2013.

XII. Appendix A: List of Commenters

1. Almond Board of California
2. American Potato Trade Alliance
3. American Soy Bean Association
4. California Table Grape Commission
5. Distilled Spirits Council of the United States
6. Grocery Manufacturers of America
7. Herbalife
8. National Confectioners Association
9. National Potato Council
10. North American Export Grain Association
11. Royal Thai Government
12. Toy Industry Association
13. Underwriters Laboratories
14. U.S. Dairy Export Council & National Milk Producers Federation
15. U.S. Wheat Associates
16. Yum! Restaurants International

XIII. Appendix B: List of Frequently Used Abbreviations and Acronyms

ANSI	American National Standards Institute
APA	Administrative Procedure Act of 1946
APEC	Asia Pacific Economic Cooperation
EU	European Union
FSCF	Food Safety Cooperation Forum
FSCF PTIN	Food Safety Cooperation Forum's Partnership Training Institute Network
FTA	Free Trade Agreement
GATT	General Agreement on Tariffs and Trade
IAF	International Accreditation Forum
IEC	International Electrotechnical Commission
ILAC	International Laboratory Accreditation Cooperation
ISO	International Organization for Standardization
MRA	Mutual Recognition Agreement
NAFTA	North American Free Trade Agreement
NAMA	Non-Agricultural Market Access
NEI	National Export Initiative
NIST	National Institute of Standards and Technology
NTTAA	National Technology Transfer and Advancement Act
NTB	Non-Tariff Barrier
NTE	National Trade Estimate Report on Foreign Trade Barriers
OECD	Organization for Economic Cooperation and Development
OMB	Office of Management and Budget
SCSC	Subcommittee on Standards and Conformance
SDO	Standards Developing Organization
SME	Small and Medium Size Enterprise
SPS	Sanitary and Phytosanitary Measures
TAA	Trade Agreements Act of 1979

TBT	Technical Barriers to Trade
TEC	United States – European Union Transatlantic Economic Council
TFTF	Trade Facilitation Task Force
TIFA	Trade and Investment Framework Agreement
TPP	Trans-Pacific Partnership
TPSC	Trade Policy Staff Committee
USDA	U.S. Department of Agriculture
USITC	U.S. International Trade Commission
USTR	Office of the United States Trade Representative
WTO	World Trade Organization